24/43

Albuquerque Academy

# OVER THE
# CHIHUAHUA AND SANTA FE
# TRAILS

# Over the Chihuahua and Santa Fe Trails 1847–1848

## George Rutledge Gibson's Journal

Edited and Annotated by
Robert W. Frazer

Published in cooperation
with the Historical Society
of New Mexico

University of New Mexico Press
Albuquerque

**Library of Congress Cataloging in Publication Data**

Gibson, George Rutledge, 1810 (ca.)–1885.
 Over the Chihuahua and Santa Fe Trails, 1847–
1848.

 "Publication in cooperation with the Historical
Society of New Mexico."
 Bibliography: p.
 1. Gibson, George Rutledge, 1810 (ca.)–1885.
2. United States—History—War with Mexico—1845
–1848—Personal narratives. 3. New Mexico—History
—War with Mexico, 1845–1848—Personal narratives.
I. Frazer, Robert Walter, 1911   . II. Historical
Society of new Mexico. III. Title.
E411.G44      973.6'2      81–52054

ISBN 0–8263–0590–3      AACR2

© 1981 by the
University of New Mexico Press.
All rights reserved.
Manufactured in the United States of America.
Library of Congress Catalog Card Number 81-52054.
International Standard Book Number 0-8263-0590-3.
First edition.

973.6
Gib
SW

# CONTENTS

24143                    Albuquerque Academy

# ILLUSTRATIONS

# Foreword

The Historical Society of New Mexico is pleased
to announce the beginning of a new series of
books devoted to the history of New Mexico. This
program is the result of a joint-publication agree-
ment between the Society and the University of
New Mexico Press. The publication of *Over the
Chihuahua and Santa Fe Trails: The Journal of George
Rutledge Gibson* is the first in this series, which we
expect will make a significant contribution to the
published history of the state.

The purpose of the history series is to publish
works on New Mexico history, emphasizing those
areas and topics which have not been published
and those which need up-dating or reprinting. It
is anticipated that this program will also stimu-
late more research and writing so that, in time, at
least two books a year will be published.

The Gibson journal is important because it is
the account of a traveller over the Santa Fe and
Chihuahua Trails during the Mexican War. It is
edited by Robert W. Frazer, a well established
scholar in the field of Southwestern history. A

portion of the journal was published previously but not the entire account. Now, for the first time, the unpublished sections are brought together and reveal Gibson's observations of life and the country of the southwest as he journeyed back from Chihuahua to Missouri.

This publication program should be the beginning of a long and mutually satisfying arrangement. The Historical Society will better fulfill one of the roles assigned to it by the Board of Directors—to increase the research and writing of New Mexico history. For its part, the University of New Mexico Press extends its commitment to contribute to the development and enjoyment of our regional culture. We look forward to a long and culturally significant relation.

The current officers and directors are:

*Officers:* Albert H. Schroeder, President; John P. Conron, Vice President; Austin Hoover, 2nd Vice President; Mrs. Hedy M. Dunn, Secretary; and Charles Bennett, Treasurer. *Directors:* Jack K. Boyer, Thomas E. Chavez, Timothy Cornish, Octavia Fellin, Dr. Myra Ellen Jenkins, Loraine Lavender, Luther L. Lyon, Morgan Nelson, Mrs. George G. Otero, Mrs. Gordon Robertson, Joe W. Stein, Michael F. Weber, Dr. Spencer Wilson, and Stephen Zimmer. *Executive Director:* Earl C. Kubicek.

John P. Conron, Chairman
Publications Committee
Historical Society of New Mexico

# Preface

George Rutledge Gibson's journal is the most extensive first-hand account by a participant in the Mexican War in New Mexico. It covers a period of approximately a year, 1846–47, followed by a gap of almost a year while Gibson resided in Santa Fe, most of that time as a civilian, and resumes when he commenced his return trip to Missouri in the spring of 1848. The two sections of the journal here presented recount his experiences in travelling from Chihuahua to Santa Fe in the spring of 1847, then, after the lapse of a year, from Santa Fe to Fort Leavenworth. Although both trips were made while the war was in progress, that contest is only incidental to Gibson's narrative. His interests extended beyond the events of the conflict and led him to comment on a variety of matters. No doubt his unflattering opinion of the Mexican people and of New Mexico's towns and villages was enhanced by the existing war and was similar to that expressed by many of his contemporaries.

Unfortunately, some of the material which

might throw additional light on aspects of the events touched on in Gibson's journal has not been located. The series of orders issued by Col. Alexander Doniphan and Col. Edward W. B. Newby during their terms of command in New Mexico have not been found in the National Archives.[1] There appear, also, to be gaps in some of the other military records of the period. Identification of characters is hampered by Gibson's failure, in most cases, to make use of given names and his occasional misspelling of surnames.

The first four sections of the journal were published in 1935 under the title *Journal of a Soldier under Kearny and Doniphan, 1846–1847* (Glendale: The Arthur H. Clark Company, Ralph P. Bieber, ed.) and reprinted in 1974 (Philadelphia: Porcupine Press). The original journal is in the possession of the Missouri Historical Society, St. Louis, Missouri, and parts five and six are published with the permission of the society. It is clear from some of Gibson's references to events which have not yet occurred at the time an entry was made that some, and perhaps all, of the journal was rewritten at a later date. Gibson's spelling has been retained but most of his abbreviations, which are not always consistent, have been spelled out. Punctuation has occasionally been altered where it was considered desirable for clarity.

1. Elmer O. Parker to R. W. Frazer, March 19, 1970.

# OVER THE
# CHIHUAHUA AND SANTA FE
# TRAILS

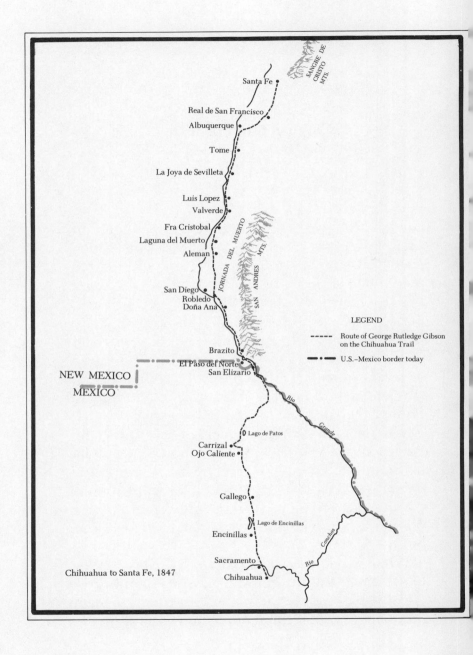

LEGEND

- - - - - Route of George Rutledge Gibson
on the Chihuahua Trail

— - — - — U.S.–Mexico border today

Santa Fe

Real de San Francisco

Albuquerque

Tome

La Joya de Sevilleta

Luis Lopez

Valverde

Fra Cristobal

Laguna del Muerto

Aleman

San Diego

Robledo

Doña Ana

Brazito

El Paso del Norte

San Elizario

NEW MEXICO

MEXICO

Lago de Patos

Carrizal

Ojo Caliente

Gallego

Lago de Encinillas

Encinillas

Sacramento

Chihuahua

JORNADA DEL MUERTO

SAN ANDRES MTS.

SANGRE DE CRISTO MTS.

Rio Grande

Rio Conchos

Chihuahua to Santa Fe, 1847

# 1

## Chihuahua to Santa Fe

George Rutledge Gibson was born, probably in 1810, in Virginia.[1] He studied law in his native state and later migrated to Vincennes, Indiana, where he opened a law office in 1834. Five years later he married Amelia Electa Hillebert of York, Illinois, and their first child was born in 1843. Gibson moved with his family to Independence, Missouri, probably in 1844. There he established a weekly newspaper, the *Independence Journal*, but suspended publication after only eight weeks. Shortly thereafter he moved to Weston, Missouri, where he again started a weekly newspaper, the *Weston Journal*, which lasted for about three and a half months. Following these financially unprofitable ventures in journalism, Gibson turned to the practice of law in Weston and was making a not too comfortable living when the Mexican War began.

When Missouri was called upon to raise volunteers for service in the war, Gibson, then thirty-six, was among the men who responded in such numbers that the initial requisition was soon exceeded. He was elected second lieutenant of the Platte County infantry company, which was mustered in at Fort Leavenworth, only seven miles from Weston, on June 27, 1846. The company became part of Col. Stephen Watts Kearny's expeditionary force, the Army of the West, destined for the occupation of New Mexico.[2] The army marched from Fort Leavenworth in detachments, Gibson's company setting out on June 29. Preceding, accompanying, and following the army were the wagons, more than four hundred of them, of the traders who were intent on pursuing their normal commerical activities in Old and New Mexico despite the existing war. Kearny's command was reunited at Bent's Fort on the north bank of the Arkansas River. On the farther side lay Mexico. Gibson and his fellows waded across, "considerably over knee-deep in some places,"[3] on August 1, thus launching their personal invasion of foreign soil. Notwithstanding all reports that New Mexico would be strongly defended, and some expressions of regret that it was not,[4] Santa Fe was occupied without opposition on August 18.

Gibson remained in Santa Fe for more than sixteen weeks but participated in none of the army movements that took so many of the troops away from the capital. By his own account, Gibson's duties were anything but onerous, giving the ex-

4

perience more the character of a casual visit. He explained a mild indisposition in October as "perhaps the effect of a good appetite and not sufficient exercise."[5] The volunteers had expected to fight a war and the novelty of living in an alien town soon disappeared. Inaction led to boredom, complaints, and, for some, drunkenness and crime. Gibson found the enforced idleness tedious and several times requested duty outside the city, but without result. This was to change, primarily because of misinformation current in Santa Fe.

Following General Kearny's departure for California on September 25, 1846, Col. Alexander Doniphan, First Missouri Mounted Volunteers, was briefly in command in Santa Fe. Col. Sterling Price arrived with the Second Regiment of Missouri Mounted Volunteers before the end of September, freeing Doniphan to conduct a brief and inconclusive campaign in the Navajo country, then to launch his invasion of Chihuahua. In November, Colonel Price decided to open communications with Brig. Gen. John E. Wool, who, it was erroneously believed, was somewhere in the vicinity of the city of Chihuahua. Price designated Lt. Col. David D. Mitchell of his own regiment to carry out the assignment and authorized him to select one hundred men from the companies stationed in Santa Fe to serve as an escort.[6]

Gibson was chosen to accompany the detachment, soon called the Chihuahua Rangers, as assistant quartermaster and commissary. The Rangers left Santa Fe early in December, Gibson departing on December 4 with the last of the baggage wagons, the weather cold and snow on the ground. He made good time down the Rio Grande and on December 16 came up with Colonel Doniphan and part of his command at Valverde,[7] the staging ground for the push across the Jornada del Muerto and the seizure of El Paso del Norte (Ciudad Juárez). Here the objective of the Rangers was changed because Doniphan simply attached the company to his expeditionary force.

Gibson took part in the Battle of Brazito[8] on Christmas Day, 1846, and the occupation of El Paso del Norte two days later. The expeditionary force remained in El Paso for six weeks, awaiting artillery reinforcements from Santa Fe and preparing to press south across the desert to Chihuahua. The delay was not unpleasant. Foodstuffs were relatively abundant in El Paso and even such luxuries as melons and fresh and dried fruits could be found in the market, not to mention wine and the much praised Pass brandy. Prices were lower than in Santa Fe, a boon to the infrequently paid troops. Gibson found the town "different from anything in New Mexico or the United States" and generally attractive.[9] He kept busy obtaining supplies to subsist his company on the march south.

At El Paso the impatient traders with more than three hundred goods-laden wagons were detained by order of Colonel Doniphan. On February 3, 1847, the Rangers were sent in pursuit of several of them who, chafing under the imposed delay, slipped away in order to get to Chihuahua and conduct their business. Most of the traders eluded the Rangers, who were soon reunited with Doniphan a short distance south of the Presidio of San Elizario.[10] The march south was largely without incident and without opposition until the army approached the hacienda of Sacramento, some twenty miles north of the city of Chihuahua. There Major General José A. Heredia, with a superior Mexican force, sought to block Doniphan's advance. Gibson was present at the Battle of Sacramento,[11] fought on February 28, and was, as were many of the others who participated in the engagement, much impressed by the grossly one-sided American victory.

Elements of Doniphan's command entered the city of Chihuahua on March 1, 1847, without further resistance. Shortly after the occupation began Gibson was relieved of his duties as quartermaster and commissary officer for the Ranger company. Colonel Mitchell, Gibson wrote, "partly at my own request and partly at his desire," ordered him back to Santa Fe. Because it was not safe to make the trip unaccompanied by a party of reasonable strength, Gibson waited until he could join a group of thirty traders returning to New Mexico. Chihuahua was held until the latter part of April when Colonel Doniphan took up his march to Saltillo, abandoning the city to its inhabitants. Even before Gibson left Chihuahua some of the troops had departed and he and his companions headed north over a completely unguarded trail toward El Paso, which had been conquered by force of arms then left entirely without an American garrison. Some of the returning traders preferred to take the longer route through Corralitos to the Santa Rita copper mines then east to strike the Santa Fe-Chihuahua road at Socorro rather than risk going through El Paso.[12]

From all indications the road between Chihuahua and El Paso carried its normal compliment of traffic as Gibson's party encountered at least one American and a number of Mexican trains coming from El Paso with goods for Chihuahua or the intervening towns. El Paso proved to be quiet, the inhabitants respectful but "cold and reserved." Gibson believed that his party, small though it was, was "too formidable" to be the object of hostile demonstrations. Once north of El Paso he apparently met very few traders. It was, of course, much too early in the year for trains from Missouri and many of the traders who had accompanied or preceded Doniphan's army were still in Old Mexico.

Gibson and Ebenezer W. Pomeroy[13] left their companions a short distance before they reached Albuquerque and took the road through Tijeras Cañon past such little settlements as Tijeras and San Antonio to New Mexico's only active gold mining district, the Old and New Placers. Gibson displayed less interest in the mines than he did in many other things and less enthusiasm for them than had some of his contemporaries.[14] He was as pleased to be back in Santa Fe after a month on the road as he had earlier been "anxious to leave" it.

The fifth section of the journal, which Gibson entitled "Journal of a Return Trip from Chihuahua to Santa Fe in the month of April 1847 In Company with a Caravan of Chihuahua Traders," follows:

*Sunday April 4 [1847]*

After the occupation of Chihuahua by Col. Donophan I was relieved by Col. Mitchel from Commissary and quarter master duties and partly at my own request and partly at his desire received an order to report to the Commanding officer at Santa Fe. Having no troops to spare for an Escort I had to wait until the 4h of April when a Company of Traders consisting of 14 wagons and thirty men were going up, which I joined expecting to reach Santa Fe about the 1st of May. All things being ready we departed on the 4h, glad we were turning our faces homewards and to the cold and healthy upper country, and came out 6 miles and camped on a Sieaka [acequia], intending to reach the Battle ground [of Sacramento] the next day. We here met Mr. Mc-Goffin[15] just getting into the city and he told us we should find grass plenty on the road, news by no means which was unpleasant. I had not been well for several weeks and having a fine riding mule and no duty to perform was in hopes I should have a return of the good health I had enjoyed since I came to the country, after getting once more on the road, without having any thing to fatigue or wear me out. We found the air much cooler than in the City and not so confined and all were in the finest spirits when we began to retrace our steps over the long and tedious road between here and our friends in the states. To Santa Fe it is about 650 miles and from there to Independence 800, making nearly 1500 miles we shall have to travel.[16]

*Monday, April 5h*
We left early and in advance of our wagons to revisit the Battle ground and examine it at our leisure, where we arrived several hours before

they did. We took a long rest at the stone corral in the bottom, where there are some cottonwoods, and then rode over the field which covers the intermediate ground between the mountains and is very extensive. The stench from the dead carcasses both of men and animals made our stay much shorter than it would have been, nor was the spectacle of a kind calculated to kindle our antipathys or resentments, for the skeletons of our Enemies were strewed over the ground, having been dragged out of their graves by the wolves, great numbers of which we saw even in the day time. They had eaten all the flesh off, but the bones were very offensive, human flesh of all others creating the most disgusting smell. This animal seems to relish it above all others, for they dug them out of the Redoubts and left the dead oxen, horses and mules almost untouched. There are still many marks of the conflict, but every thing of the least value has been carried away. How they could suffer so small a force to take such a Post looks strange, especially with the loss of only two men,[17] and the Traveller in future will regard it as one of the most brilliant acts on record. By the time our curiosity was satisfied, the wagons came up and we encamped, considering ourselves now fairly on the road and every thing going on extremely well. The wolves at night set up a most dismal howl and seemed to be gathered from the whole country to enjoy the rare and unusual feast they have had for a month past.

*Tuesday April 6h*

Our wagons were light, and we intended to make a short trip, and took this morning an early start, first having a cup of coffee to warm us. We now left, many of us perhaps for the last time, a piece of ground which History will make celebrated, and came to the Piñon[18] where we watered our animals, and then proceeded on to the Piñolite where we camped, about 18 or 20 miles from Sacramento. At the Ranche[19] we met a number of Corretas from El Passo loaded with the productions of that place, but having left a fiew days after our Battle, they could give us no news later than we had from Mr. McGoffin. I found several acquaintances amongst them, one the alcalde of the Presidio [of San Elizario] who seemed glad to see me and gave us agua ardienti [aguardiente, very possibly Pass brandy]. At night a number of other corretas from the same place passed, their creaking making night hideous and driving sleep from every living creature in miles around. Had Don Quixote heard a caravan of these rude wagons, or Sancho Panza been near more fearful consequences would have followed than did to these two veritable heroes, from the noise of the fulling mills. As it was our rest was disturbed, nothing more. The water here is good and near to the Road, being a clear, running stream which empties into the Lake [Encinillas], but grass was very scarce and we had to rely entirely upon the corn which we brought from the City, being well provided for in this respect. There is also plenty of Muskeet for fuel of a large size.

### Wednesday April 7

We made an early start this morning to reach the head of the Lake, 25 miles, thus in one day travelling double the distance we did coming down. In 8 miles we came to the Piñon again and here struck the Burnt District,[20] extending to the Gaiaga spring,[21] a distance of 45 miles, but the young grass had sprung up, which afforded a scanty pasturage for our animals, and we were better off than we expected. After a siesta in my Tent which is very comfortable and useful in the heat of the day and several hours rest, we continued up the Lake to camp which we reached in good season, abundance of Ducks, Geese, Cranes etc being visible, but beyond our reach. The scenery around here is amongst the finest I have seen, some of the mountains rising to a considerable elevation, but like the whole range, they lack variety to give to them that interest which one takes in the Alleghaney chain or more Northern part of the Rocky Mountain. Mr. Pomeroy[22] messes with us, one of our Sutlers, and I find him an agreeable and pleasant companion—and we have in company Mr. Hoffman[23] from Baltimore, and Mr. Ewing[24] from Lexington Mo. The Three are specimens of American character deserving of notice. One had spent a part of his life in Oregon, another had made the Tour of Europe and gone even as far as St. Petersburgh and the third had resided in the West Indies. Of course all these places and countries are frequent subjects of conversation as we ride along and afford one another interest which nothing else could supply, being usually by ourselves in the advance of our wagons.

*Friday April 9h*

The morning was disagreeably cold and although it was intended to enter the *Jornada*[25] very nearly we found ourselves still at camp when the Sun peered over the mountains at the base of which we lay. We rode along in advance for several miles and espied two men coming toward us, which of course in the wilds always raises many speculations as to who they are and in this case we were in hopes it would prove to be an Express with the mail, and Letters from our friends. But they turned out to be men in advance of 20 Coretas and wagons and about 60 men from El Passo on their way to Chihuahua with the productions of that place, the creaking of these vehicles giving notice of their approach almost as far as the eyes can reach. They always go in large parties on account of the Apaches who infest the whole road and are armed as well as Mexicans usually are. I noticed many women along, who seem on all trading expeditions to accompany the men, and several were very good looking. We passed each other without stopping as they had been a long time out and had no news. After 15 miles travel we camped to noon it and made a hearty Dinner, our Rabbit having furnished us with a breakfast. We also sent our animals 2 1/2 miles to a spring in a deep Cañon in the mountains for water and now only have about 40 miles without this indispensible article to pass over. After our siesta we continued on until 12 oclock at night and camped with grass in abundance, and chomisa, muskeet, oil weed etc for fuel. Nearly all the men were too much fatigued to cook supper, but I prefered remaining up until I got a cup of coffee and then foll[ow]ed them to my blankets, where I had a comfortable nights rest.

*Saturday April 10h*

We broke up camp late having to put a tire on a wheel which [the tire] came off last night 2 miles from camp. The climate is so dry that great care has to be observed about things of this kind and even trunks which in the States last a long time soon come to pieces, or other wood work of any kind. The morning was warm and the road very dusty but we arrived early at the Ojo Caliente,[26] where we camped with wood, water and grass. Of course we all enjoyed the Luxury of a bath in this celebrated spring and found it both pleasant and necessary as we were not very clean after travelling 140 miles over sandy and dusty roads, with scarcely enough water to drink and cook, much less to wash our hands and faces. The Pool, made by the first explorers of the Country, contains many fish and we amused ourselves in the afternoon angling for the finny tribe and succeeded in procuring enough for supper which we found very fine. The day was as pleasant as could be wished for and having determined to remain all night to recruit our animals we spent the evening reading, Mr. Hoffman having brought for his own use several Books. Agnes Serle by Mrs. Pickering[27] fell to my share, which I found interesting and it was quite a novelty to sit down in the wilds on the banks of a clear spring branch and read one of the latest and most fashionable novels of the day. The want of Books to read at our leisure moments has been a source of great annoyance since we first came into the country, a vexation which has to be experienced to appreciate.

*Sunday April 11*
  We left the spring this morning with reluctance and would have been glad if we could have taken it along, and continued our march to Carisal,[28] 12

miles, where we encamped on the Sieaka to noon it, all going into Town to purchase provisions. By hunting all over it we succeeded in obtaining Eggs, a fiew chickens, and several small Pigs, these being all the Eatible things which the Town could raise, though there are at least 200 Lousey, Lazy and ragged men to be seen about the streets, part of which were at Sacramento as they told us and amongst the rest a Captain. It is astonishing to see how little these people live upon, and yet if given to them I have never found greater gluttons, but they are too ignorent and Lazy to keep themselves well provided and seem to put up with the little Providence throws in their way. They loose nothing of a hog or Beef, head, feet, Entrails and all being carefully saved and eaten, a small piece of meat, *chili Colorado*, Beans, and tortillas constituting their daily repast which last 24 hours except a cup of chocolate and piece of bread. They will travel for days on Atole or Piñole or parched corn, and retain their health, looks and activity and shew no symptoms of hunger at the end of the time. After taking our siesta we continued our march to within 6 miles of the Laguna De Los Patos,[29] having travelled altogether today about 25 miles. I saw a specimen of Mexican art here which would astonish our market women, done by a fat greasy looking girl, but it will not do to go on paper, nor am I sure it would be believed. But it beats the old story of driving hens up hill.

*Monday April 12h*

We left early and went to the Laguna De Los Patos for Breakfast, which place we reached at 9 oclock and remained there until half past four, intending to enter the Cantaresio Jornada[30] at this hour, which we did, passing the Oho Lusero[31] about dark. Whilst at the Laguna an *Atajo* [train] of Pack mules came up on their way to Corisal from whom we procured vino and some fruits, which were by no means unpleasant on the road. The weather was very warm and our Road a good one, so we continued on it all night in preference to the day to save our animals and

*Tuesday April 13*

about 9 oclock in the morning arrived at the Cantaresio 30 miles from the Laguna. We met at the gap in the mountains about midnight several wagons from the Pass loaded for Chihuahua belonging to Don Poncé[32] but being night we passed each other with out obtaining any information. Last night was warm and to day we have August weather with exceedingly dusty roads. After our usual Siesta we left the Cantaresio at half past four in the Evening having 25 miles of sandy, broken road to pass over before we reach the Rio Grande, our animals needing water very much. To night however was pleasant and about 12 oclock or later we all encamped in the bottom on this stream once more, very glad to find ourselves through two of the three Jornadas on our route, this last one being particularly severe, from bad roads, the great quantity of dust, and the length, 65 miles without water or any wood except a little muskeet which we have to burn green and consequently is not very good.

*Wednesday April 14h*

The day is very warm, all puffing and blowing and dreaming of Mint Julips, Ice creams, Lemonades and the Luxuries in our Country and we remained in camp until Evening resting ourselves and animals after the hard march. Our servants went fishing and brought in three Large Cat fish, two weighing above five pounds each, and of course we are pleased as we have been living upon the remains of a Grunter which we purchased at Corisal and which is neither wholesome nor palatable on a march. At 4 oclock we took the road again and found it better than the one we came down, having crossed over a fiew miles above camp to the Island[33] which extends nearly to El Passo. We kept up the Island with very pretty groves of cotton woods, the soil rich and the grass, young, green and abundant and in 8 miles camped on the Bank of the River. Soon after reaching camp it became very windy and in a short time clouded up, with every appearance of Rain, but the next morning we found ourselves only covered with dust and sand. There is but

19

one Tent in Company and that is mine, which Mr. Pomeroy sleeps in being an invalid, I myself preferring from long habit to sleep in the open air and all the others do the same from necessity. The Tent however is very servicible to me when we stop to noon it to keep off the Hot Sun, which at this season of the year is oppressive in this climate. A fiew fish were caught again this Evening but we are still supplied with fresh meat and have no anxiety on that score now.

*Friday April 16h*

Mr. Pomeroy has contracted for a quantity of vino and agua ardiente at El Passo and we went in advance this morning with one wagon and the barrels to have them filled ready by the time the others came up, the others remaining in camp where it was intended to procure corn, Beef and a fiew other things we needed and which it was feared could not be had at El Passo, our camp being in the Place called Socorro.[34]

Early in the day we took lodgings at the Casa of Mrs. McKnight[35] and visited some of our acquaintances, all of whom we found well and tried to pick up a little news from Santa Fe but learned nothing.

The place seems dull to what it did as we went down and the streets almost deserted, but it still is a pleasant place and with its vineyards, and fruit trees and shrubbery a pretty place. The people are respectful but by no means generally manifested a warm feeling towards us, being cold and reserved. The news of General [Zachary] Taylor's victory [in the Battle of Buena Vista ] is [far] from cheering them up and they are dispirited, the women alone retaining their volubility and kindness. I saw the Padre Ortis,[36] he looks care worn and no doubt feels very sensibly the position he is placed in and would be glad to have an opportunity to change it. He would cut all of our throats if he could do so, but our little party is too formidable to be dealt with roughly and as they desire.

*Saturday April 17*

We remained here for the wagons, which arrived early in the day, and in the mean time procured such things as we could get and settled the little business on our hands. I saw Mr. Jacques[37] at whose Casa I boarded awhile [on the way south] and he embraced me warmly and manifested a personal friendship which I returned. But like all Mexicans he is tricky and I watched him closely without being able to discover anything. The Prefect [Sebastián Bermúdez] swindled me in some wine I bought to take home as a sample of the country, and when the highest Civil officer can do such a thing it is time to keep an eye upon every one.

The People are all busy planting corn and the season appears to me three weeks later here than at Chihuahua; perhaps more even than that. The cotton woods do not wear the summer hue they had below though we are two weeks out, nor is the weather so warm, nor has the sun such a blinding glare, nor does the Maguey flourish here as in Chihuahua. The atmosphere is also damper on the River than the small streams which flow from the mountains as tributaries to it, which we felt very sensibly as we approached the Rio Grande, at least five or six miles off.

All things being ready we left late in the evening, having scarcely time to cross the River when we encamped, and saw several sky Rockets thrown up in the Town, about which there were many speculations. The General opinion was that Padre Ortis had received intelligence of some kind which caused rejoicing but I attributed it to some other cause and it turned out to be a frolic of the boys.

*Sunday April 18h*

Just as we were making preparations to start, my friend Leandro Gomez[38] came into camp loaded down with presents of vino, bread, grapes, onion seed etc which he had taken the trouble to bring 7 or 8 miles and I in return had to make him presents of tobacco and sugar. I purchased also from him a gourd such as is generally used in the country in place of canteens and we parted as good friends as ever.

After some detention for a fiew things which had been left in Town and were sent for, we proceeded on our way, and after stopping a while at Ponces Ranche,[39] soon left the bottoms and ascended the hills or mountains, if they deserve the name, which line both sides of the River and give the name of Pass.

The River here runs through a sort of Cañon for several miles, the mountains on each side extending to the waters edge and it looks [as] if it had required a convulsion of nature to open the channel. Instead of following the road we took a path which led directly up its Banks over the most broken and romantic spot I had seen in the country, being compelled often to dismount and lead our mules down the precipices, where the slip of a foot might have precipitated them into the River. The whole country is very rocky and of volcanic origen and I saw several species of Palmetto[40] new to us and many others in full bloom, the flowers very large and rich. After getting through this a distance of 9 miles from El Passo we struck the bottom again and encamped, the wagons not getting up until late and the mules much worsted, there being no road between Chihuahua and Santa Fe so bad, or so broken.

*Monday April 19*

The Prarie wolves tried to take our camp this morning running the Dogs several times amongst the wagons, and the men fired on them several times but failed to kill any. A fine noble Cur belonging to Mr. Pomeroy was run over yesterday evening by a wagon and is left behind. We all took great interest in Cassius as Mr. Pomeroy more than a year since lost him in Texas and found him at Sacramento, each at once recognizing the other. He no doubt was stolen and brought to Chihuahua by the Camanches and there left.

We preceded the wagons to Lagunita[41] where we reposed until they came up, when we went on and camped 12 miles from the River at the Pass. Late in the evening we resumed our march, and just as we were about to drive off, our old friend and acquaintance Don Ponce came up, when an amusing scene took place between him and two greaser[42] women he claimed as his servants who had induced a Teamster to bring them thus far on their road to the upper country, absconding no doubt. Mr. Ponce succeeded though in regaining them from the driver, who manifested a disposition to take their part, and we came on to the Battle Ground of Brazito and encamped just before dark, having made altogether today 18 miles. We here saw still some evidence of the conflict and looked with great interest at a place where several of our company had been engaged with the Enemy.

Frank this evening caught another catfish, so that we shall still have this Luxury in the absence of other fresh meat.

## *Tuesday April 20h*

We left camp early with a long, level bottom before us when we again struck the River, and camped to noon it, and in the evening resumed our march and continued on the Road until we reached the Sieaka two miles from Doña Anna, where we remained all night. Several of us in advance of the wagons went to town where we met our friend Miranda,[43] and returned in the evening. We found corn in abundance at $3. per Fanega and the people better disposed than on any part of the Road. It was late when the teams came up, the road being heavy sand, but vino kept our spirits up until we reached camp when we found our blankets the most comfortable place we had. We met today two wagons from Socorro[44] with tobacco for Mr. Pomeroy who received it and they turned back, having been delayed too long on the road. Our transportation is consequently greatly increased. We we [sic] think we can get along well. This [Doña Ana] is one of the fiew places which bears marks of improving and is well situated, and has water in abundance.[45]

Being now claimed as American soil its two proprietors, Ponce and Miranda, will probably keep it advancing in wealth and resources and make a respectable place.

*Wednesday April 21st*

Early in the morning we moved into town and remained there until evening, procuring corn and such other things as we stood in need of. Miranda was lavish of his hospitality and receives from all great respect for his gentlemanly deportment. He expressed great regret for the death of Col. [Samuel C.] Owen. He also pointed out to me two Mexican Dragoons in his employment who were at Sacramento and had exchanged the Sabre for the Plowshare.

In the afternoon we had an alarm that the apaches were driving off our stock and the house tops were crowded with the population, but the men who first went out returned and reported they could find none and quiet was restored.

There is a pretty chain of mountains, nearly opposite the town, called Los Organos, being a continuation of the chain from Fra Christobal. This is a hasty sketch of them taken above town on the Bank of the River.

After procuring supplies of corn and provisions we marched and camped for the night in a Bottom four miles above town where the grass was very green and abundant, and more like our own

... ly opposite the town called Los Organos ...
intimation of the choir from Jira Christ
is a treaty Sketch of them taken above I
the Bank of the River —

... for procuring supplies of corn and provisions
... and on and camped for the night in a boat
miles above town where the grup was very
abundant, and more like our own green gra...
any thing we have seen — the evening was

green fields than any thing we have seen. The evening was delightful and we congregated under the shade of an old cotton wood on the mother earth and spent an hour or two very pleasantly.

*Thursday April 22d*

The air this morning was cool enough to make a Blanket or great coat comfortable, and our climate has evidently changed, being now similar to the Rattone [Raton Pass]. We took an early start though and came to Roblero[46] where we nooned it and repaired a wagon which had sustained some damage and in the Evening travelled to San Diago[47] which we reached about 10 oclock at night, making our days work 25 miles.

Just before camping we met two mexicans who said they were from Santa Fe, but they had no mail and could give us no news except that the Navijos were again committing depredations on the Rio Abajo. We let them pass on, but wished afterwards we had detained them and examined them for letters, as we have concluded they were sent as a private express by the disaffected in this Territory and since reaching Santa Fe such we learn is probably their business, one of them at least being known as an instigator in the late troubles.[48]

The line which separates Chihuahua from New Mexico runs a little south of our present camp (about Roblero) but we claim all this side of the River and difficulties may some day grow out of the uncertain boundary. The Los Organos, Los Animas, and the Copper mine mountains[49] all being in the one or the other state as the boundary may be settled. The latter are valuable on account of their mineral resources and it is desirable our Government should have them as a part of New Mexico.

### Friday April 23

We remained in camp until 4 oclock in the Evening intending to enter the much dreaded *Jornad del Muerto* at that hour, and in the mean time sent our animals to the River for water, under a strong guard, at least 2 miles off, as we have 85 miles to pass over without any prospect of this indispensible article. Our wood we necessarily had to lay in at Roblero even for our present camp as well as water in our casks. All things being ready we broke up camp and started on this high and dry plain and continued to travel at a good gait until 2 oclock at night when we stopped near the Alleman,[50] having made 40 miles. We found the grass here abundant and good and we remained a fiew hours to refresh our animals and let them pick a little, not having stopped on the road a moment previous to this.

### Saturday April 24h

As soon as it was light enough to geer up we started again without breakfast and in 15 miles came to the Laguna del Muerto[51] which is perfectly dry and camped, cooked, and sent our animals for water to the Oho Del Muerto,[52] distant 3 miles, in charge of half the company.

Yesterday evening we had a severe storm of wind and dust, which blew up suddenly as we passed the Pasea and Point of Rocks,[53] with a sudden change in the weather which made our great Coats comfortable. These Blow though seldom accompanied with rain are very unpleasant and resemble at a distance from the dust a violent storm of wind and rain, and even have often thunder and Lightning.

Today we passed over a section where rain had fallen but the only good it did us was to lay the dust and moisten the grass which our animals eat with avidity, there were no pools, no standing water for our animals.

At 4 oclock we again took the road and travelled until late at night, probably 4 oclock in the morning, when we found ourselves within 2 miles of the River and again encamped, having come 85 miles in 36 hours besides the 14 our animals had to pass over to get water, and this too with wagons loaded with 4500 lbs. Mr. Ewing and Hoffman though could not keep up and their teams stopped 8 miles back of us intending to overtake us the next day at Fra Christobal[54] at which we shall remain to recruit our animals. We had the good luck to have both moonshine and cool weather to pass over this road and as we advance find the rain which fell yesterday much heavier here than back, the ground being in some places muddy. Just before Day Light we lay down to get a little sleep, having been up the last two nights and soon forgot our cares except when some noisy Teamsters made us open our lids to see what was the matter. The next two miles is over broken and bad roads and we stopped here partly on this account and more because the grass is better than in the bottoms, there being nothing for miles superior to the Gramma grass on the Hills.

*Sunday April 25h*

After Breakfast we moved our camp about three miles to the River, intending to remain there to day to recruit our animals after the hard march through the *Jornada* and stopped at a pretty place, of which I made a hasty sketch made at camp.

We hear frogs this evening for the first time, not having seen such an animal on the whole road and but fiew snakes, probably for the reason there is so little water on it.

We found at Fra Christobal several large flocks of sheep and goats in charge of herders or Shepards from whom we purchased about a dozen head and now have mutton again. In the evening we were threatened with a storm, several of which passed around the different mountains in our view, but we escaped. The ground bears evidence and stopped at a pretty place, of which I made a hasty ske- made at camp—

River

Camp

Road ——— Ina-Christobal

we heard frogs this evening for the first time, not having seen such an animal on the whole road and find them snakes, probably for the reason there is so little of a hard rain having fallen lately, almost the first since we left El Passo, having had but one rain from El Passo to Chihuahua and back again.

## Monday April 26

The morning was cloudy, damp and cold enough to require us to draw on our great coats, weather which is rather unusual in this climate at this season of the year, it being too soon by 6 weeks for the rainy season. We left early and in 9 miles came to the pretty *mesa* below Val Verde bottom, but concluding it best to pass over the bad road before we stop, which extends the other side of the mesa, we kept on and nooned it in the bottom having made 12 miles. It continued cloudy all day, but we had no rain and late in the Evening the sun came out and after travelling 8 or 10 miles camped for the night one mile above the Ford on the Socorro road where we had wood, water and grass and a pretty camp in the Cotton Woods. We were compelled to keep up this side of the River on account of high water, the rains or snows having raised it enough to prevent crossing with wagons. Altogether we travelled to day 18 or 20 miles and tomorrow will be in the settlements in New Mexico but would have preferred going by Socorro.

## Tuesday April 27h

We left camp early and after a tedious march of 15 miles over bad roads, up a sandy bottom came to the first settlement, a new and small place, called, I believe, San Pedro[55] where we nooned it and procured a fiew chickens and Eggs, this being all the wretched, ignorant, dirty, and poor people had. In the Evening we made about 5 miles over Sieakas, passing the Bosque Sieta[56] where we procured vino to enliven us. It was after dark when we encamped, the last 2 miles very bad road, sandy and hilly. Duck, Geese etc plenty but wild and we took no great pains to get any. Our days travel was 20 miles.

*Wednesday April 28h*

We made an early start, but a short days journey having been detained at Caneda,[57] a small town, to load 20 fanegas of corn for the teams. We stopped at the Alcalde's where a pretty girl was much pleased because Mr. Pomeroy's Negro boy "Tom" gave her a lock of his curly hair and we found all the balance of the population of course poor, ignorant, and dirty; we succeeded however in procuring a fiew Eggs and chickens and vino, which helped our meals. Our days journey was only 8 miles.

*Thursday April 29h*

We had not proceeded many miles upon our road today before we met Mr. Biggs[58] from Placere[59] on his way to El Passo with several wagons. He first informed us of Capt. Moore's, Capt. Johnson's, and Lt. Hammond's[60] deathes in California and Genl. Kearney's troubles and several other little pieces of news, but they had no mail or papers. Mr. Pomeroy killed 2 ducks and we promise ourselves a good dinner tomorrow. We passed through La Joya Sivollette[61] where as usual Eggs, chickens, and vino was all we could procure and after travelling today about 20 miles camped without wood or grass for which our animals are suffering, having had none today.

*Friday April 30*

We left camp early and had [a] very bad road but travelled 20 miles and camped just below Toma [Tomé] where we met Mr. Powers[62] from Santa Fe with 2 wagons on his way to El Passo. He remained with us all night and gave us the particulars of the disturbances and fights in this section which were of great interest. For the first time I learned from him that Lt. Van Valken-burgh[63] of my company was killed at the head of the Company gallantly fighting, than whom there was no better soldier or man. We set up until late, all these things interesting us very much and at last after collecting all the news he could give us retired to our blankets.

*Saturday May 1st*

We made an early start and in 3 miles entered Toma through which we passed without stop-ping, seeing nothing to entice us to do so and in a fiew miles more passed through another settlement [Valencia] and in 6 miles came to Peralto where we stopped and were hospitably entertained by our friends Genl. Pratt,[64] Mr. Quinn[65] and Mr. Skinner,[66] the Sheriff, Clerk, and District Attorney. They related to us many incidents of interest which had occurred in our absence, and we spent a very pleasant time at their casa. After dinner we followed the wagons, which we found grased up ready to start and travelled about 8 miles on the Placere Road when we encamped at 10 oclock at night, the wind and cold very unpleasant, as we neither had wood, water, nor much grass, except what we hawled. Mr. Robinson[67] with 5 wagons fell behind today and camped just this side of Peralto on account of the sand hills [he] had to pass over. We travelled about 20 miles.

*Sunday May 2d*

Early in the morning we were on the road which is directly to the Placere [Ortiz] Mountains over a high, dry Table land about 7 miles distant, with the air very chilly and disagreeable, and camped at the mouth of a Cañon to noon it, on a small stream, where we found many indications that we had reached the mineral region. Whilst nooning the wind calmed off, and the weather was pleasant and after taking our usual siesta Mr. Pomeroy and myself left the company for Placere, wishing to see the Gold mines, our road for 7 or 8 miles being up the Cañon, the mountains on each side very rocky, precipitous and picture[s]que, with large pine and cedar, the first we have met with since we left Santa Fe. After travelling 15 miles (altogether about 25) and passing several settlements,[68] we found ourselves belated, and not knowing the road, nor how far we still were from Placere we stopped about an hour after night in a pretty grove of Pine and Cedar, kindled a large fire and with some cold bread and meat made our supper, our animals as usual being picketed out with but little grass. Requiring Rest, with our Saddle Blankets and great coats we each made a bed and fared well until midnight when the wind blew a gale and was cold and chilly, so that we were not rendered effeminate by being over comfortable and had only a tolerable nights rest being very deficient in the comforts of a house.

*Monday May 3*

Our situation not being the most comfortable we left early to reach Placere [actually the mining village of Real de San Francisco, now Golden] where we expected to be able to procure something and in 5 or 6 miles came to this little mining town, which we found deserted by the mexican population. We stopped and fed our animals at Mr. Campbell's[69] who has a well assorted stock of goods and is the only one now whose mine is worked. We learned from him that the mines had not been worked since the late Rebellion

[Taos uprising] when they deserted them and joined the insurgents. He told us they usually worked from 500 to 2500 men and now had only about 40 and he did not expect them to return before winter. The whole country wears a mineral aspect, and some is procured by washing and some by the different other ways known. The town is a poor looking place, nothing but mean huts in the mountains and does not indicate its proximity to the precious metals. We were satisfied without examining further and soon after leaving, which we did early, though invited to remain for breakfast, came in sight of the Mountains North of Santa Fe, their snowy summits glittering in the sun and presenting a novel sight to men just from the sunny south, the air at the same time being evidently cooler and more bracing. We nooned it at Galisteo creek, 12 miles from Placere, where the remainder of our cold bread and meat furnished a meal and then continued on to Santa Fe which we reached at Sun Down having traveled 40 miles. My own Company did not know me, I had been so altered by Sombrero, whiskers, and a change of dress, but crowds now collected around me to greet and inquire the news, which pleased them very much.

*Wednesday May 5h*

Instead of finding Col. Price advised of what had been done at Washington and of what he was expected to accomplish I found there had been no mail since February and I determined to await the arrival of one, the state of things being such as to require it, consequently the traders go on without me. I was in hopes I should find several letters in the office but there were none and I have to put up with what I cant help.

The mountains all around are covered with snow and it looks like winter though the air is only a little chilly here in town. We could see it snowing yesterday.

I visited the Fort [70] and was not only astonished but grieved at its [the post cemetery's] magnitude. 300 new made graves attest the mortality which existed amongst the troops and teamsters and three little hillocks on the side of the hill mark the spot where Gov. [Charles] Bent, Capt. [John H. K.] Burgwin and A[lbert]. G. Wilson repose.[71] It is a melancholy spectacle to visit the ground and [it] is already an extensive Grave Yard. Various causes brought the men to an untimely end. Some from dissipation. Some from Exposure. Some the want of attention. Some broken down constitutions. Some from fever and some from the effects of colds. The health of the army here though I found good at this time, the weak and sickly having pretty much all died off. Measles was also a fruitful disease in filling up the ground.[72]

# Notes

## Chapter 1

1. For a biographical sketch of Gibson see Ralph P. Bieber, ed., *Journal of a Soldier Under Kearny and Doniphan, 1846–1847* (Glendale, 1935), pp. 17–21, 35–36, 102–7.

2. The organization of the volunteers is discussed in Dwight L. Clarke, *Stephen Watts Kearny, Soldier of the West* (Norman, 1961), pp. 106–11. Kearny was promoted to the rank of Brigadier General when the army marched from Fort Leavenworth.

3. Gibson, *Journal*, p. 173.

4. John T. Hughes, *Doniphan's Expedition* (Cincinnati, 1849), p. 72.

5. Gibson, *Journal*, p. 262.

6. O, No. 71, November 17, 1846, Record Group (RG) 94, Records of the Office of the Adjutant General (OAG), Orders and Special Orders, Army in New Mexico, The National Archives, Washington, D. C.

7. At this time Valverde was simply a camping place, *paraje*, near the northern end of the Jornada del Muerto.

8. There has been some question as to the exact site of the Battle of Brazito. See George Ruhlen, "The Battle of Brazito—Where It Was Fought," *Password*, II (May, 1957), 53–60. Estimates of the number of Mexican troops engaged vary from 500 to 1220. Doniphan reported that he had 856 effective men. The known number of Mexican dead was 43 while Doniphan's casualties were limited to 7 wounded, all of whom recovered. Report of Secretary of War William L. Marcy, 30 Cong., 1 Sess., Sen. Exec. Doc. 1, I, 498.

9. Gibson, *Journal,* pp. 312–13. The Americans generally were impressed by El Paso. One private wrote, "El Paso is in fact an extensive vineyard, and must in the summer be one of the most delightful places in the world." Jacob S. Robinson, *A Journal of the Santa Fe Expedition Under Colonel Doniphan* (Princeton, 1932), p. 69.

10. The Presidio of San Elizario was located at the southern end of the island in the Rio Grande below El Paso del Norte. It was established in 1773. In 1849 it was occupied as a military post by the United States.

11. According to John T. Hughes, American losses in the battle were one dead and eleven wounded, three of whom died later. *Doniphan's Expedition,* p. 313. The number of Mexicans killed is usually put at about three hundred.

12. James J. Webb, *Adventures in the Santa Fé Trade, 1844–1847,* Ralph P. Bieber, ed. (Glendale, 1931), p. 281.

13. Ebenezer W. Pomeroy of Lexington, Missouri, was a prominent trader who had served as sutler with Doniphan's expedition on the march to Chihuahua. When James Aull, who had been in partnership with Samuel C. Owens (see n. 17) was killed by Mexicans in his Chihuahua store in June, 1847, Pomeroy and three other traders went to Chihuahua to take charge of Aull's property. Pomeroy left Santa Fe in August and did not return to Missouri until July, 1848. Max Moorhead, *New Mexico's Royal Road* (Norman, 1954), p. 182; and Louise Barry, *The Beginning of the West* (Topeka, 1972), p. 762.

14. See, for example, James W. Abert, *Abert's New Mexico Report, 1846–47* (Albuquerque, 1962), pp. 49–52; and Adolph Wislizenus, *Memoir of a Tour to Northern Mexico* (Albuquerque, 1969), pp. 30–33.

15. This was Samuel Magoffin, who, with his wife Susan Shelby Magoffin, was en route to Chihuahua with other traders. They had left El Paso on March 14. Unfortunately, Mrs. Magoffin made no entries in her diary between April 1 and May 23, 1847. *Down the Santa Fe Trail and into Mexico,* Stella M. Drumm, ed. (New Haven, 1926), pp. 223, 228.

16. Gibson overestimated the total distance by about 150 miles.

17. Major Samuel C. Owens, who commanded the battalion organized among the traders, two companies of seventy-five men each, was killed in the battle. A native of Kentucky, Owens moved to Missouri as a young man and was one of the founders of Independence. He participated prominently in both business and politics and had made at least one earlier trip to New Mexico. Webb, *Adventures in the Santa Fé Trade*, p. 42n. Gibson's reference to a second death may be to that of a sergeant who died of wounds immediately after the battle.

18. On his way south Gibson described the Piñon (Peñón) as "a small lake of muddy water, which is also brackish." *Journal*, p. 343. None of the contemporary accounts consulted mention the "Piñolite." From the text of the journal it appears to be a stream flowing into the Laguna de Encinillas.

19. The Hacienda del Peñol was the property of General Angel Trías, governor of Chihuahua at the time of Doniphan's invasion.

20. The "burnt district" was the result of a grass fire, started inadvertently by Doniphan's command on the march south which burned unchecked over an extensive area. Hughes, *Doniphan's Expedition*, pp. 297–99. Gibson wrote that the fire started in Major William Gilpin's camp. *Journal*, p. 339.

21. On the way south Gibson called the spring the "Gaigeta" and placed it two miles south of the better known Ojo de Gallego. *Journal*, p. 339. Hughes called it Guyagas Springs. *Doniphan's Expedition*, p. 296.

22. See n. 13.

23. J. Tilghman Hoffman of Baltimore was described as "a very small and feeble man, [with a] dark complexion." Webb, *Adventures in the Santa Fe Trade*, p. 211. He left Santa Fe on May 18, 1847, and returned to the States via Taos and Bent's Fort, reaching Westport, Missouri, on June 9. Barry, *Beginning of the West*, pp. 627, 690.

24. Ewing, probably Finis Y. Ewing, went on immediately from Santa Fe to Missouri, carrying $16,000 entrusted to him by Pomeroy. Barry, *Beginning of the West*, p. 669.

25. The Jornada de Jesús María was the first of three extensive, relatively waterless segments of the route between Chihuahua and Santa Fe. Moorhead, *New Mexico's Royal Road*, p. 115.

26. Wislizenus, who visited the Ojo Caliente in August 1846, wrote, "it is a clear, pure water, in a large basin of porphyritic rocks, with sandy bottom, out of which many warm springs come to the surface. The thermometer placed in the spring, showed 82° Fah,; the atmosphere, 84.50°." *Memoir of a Tour*, p. 45. The springs were described by almost all diarists who saw them and some, as did Gibson, attributed the natural pools to the work of man.

27. Ellen Pickering published at least ten novels, some of which apparently were juveniles. *Agnes Serle* was published c. 1830 by G. B. Zieber and Co., Philadelphia, and so was not as recent as Gibson implied.

28. Carrizal was originally a hacienda that was abandoned early in the eighteenth century because of Apache attacks. The pueblo was established in 1758, and protection was provided by a small garrison from the presidio at El Paso del Norte. Eleanor B. Adams, ed., *Bishop Tameron's Visitation of New Mexico, 1760* (Albuquerque, 1954), p. 39. The presidio was transferred from El Paso to Carrizal shortly after 1773.

29. The Lago de Patos, shallow, brackish, and marshy, is the outlet of the Río del Carmen and does not itself have an outlet.

30. The Jornada de Cantarrecio avoided the worst of the sand dunes which were crossed by the route leading directly south from El Paso del Norte and so was favored for heavily loaded wagons. It was not entirely without sources of water. Moorhead, *New Mexico's Royal Road*, pp. 114–15. Gibson, considering that the Jornada ended at the Rio Grande, gave its length as sixty-five miles. *Journal*, p. 332.

31. The Ojo Lucero was described by Wislizenus as "a fine spring. . . . The Water comes out of a small, sandy basin in the prairie, but with considerable force; it is clear and soft of taste; the temperature of the spring was 77.5°

Fah., while the atmosphere in the shade was 81° Fah."
*Memoir of a Tour,* p. 26.

32. Juan María Ponce de León was reputed to be the wealthiest man in El Paso del Norte at this time, with an income of about $10,000 per year. He owned property on both sides of the Rio Grande. His grant north of the river, which Americans usually referred to as Ponce's Ranch, embraced the site on which El Paso, Texas, was later established. Frank S. Edwards, *A Campaign in New Mexico with Colonel Doniphan* (Philadelphia, 1847), p. 91; and C. L. Sonnichsen, *Pass of the North* (El Paso, 1968), p. 107. Edwards was Gibson's assistant; that is, quartermaster sergeant in the Chihuahua Rangers.

33. At this time the Rio Grande divided below El Paso del Norte and flowed through two channels, thus creating an island about thirty miles long and one to four miles wide on which there were three settlements, Socorro del Sur, Isleta del Sur, and San Elizario (originally a presidio). The island was cultivated throughout its extent and was famed for its production. William S. Henry to Lafayette McLaws, February 20, 1850, RG 98, Records of United States Army Commands, Department of New Mexico, Letters Received. The Rio Grande has since changed its course and the island is now part of its left bank.

34. Socorro del Sur was established by Governor Antonio de Otermín as a settlement for some of the Pueblo Indians who fled south with the Spaniards at the time of the Pueblo Revolt of 1680. It was named for the Piro pueblo of Socorro, New Mexico, and, presumably, was populated largely by refugees from that pueblo. By Gibson's day it was partly Mexicanized.

35. Mrs. McKnight has not been identified.

36. Padre Ramón Ortiz was a curate in El Paso del Norte. Some years earlier he had befriended the the Texans who were taken prisoner in the so-called Texan-Santa Fe expedition. Colonel Doniphan, who distrusted him, took him as a hostage to Chihuahua, where he was released. Hughes, *Doniphan's Expedition,* pp. 288, 325. See also Thomas Fal-

coner, *Letters and Notes on the Texan Santa Fe Expedition, 1841–1842* (New York, 1930), p. 98.

37. Gibson wrote that Pedro Jacques belonged to "one of the best families" of El Paso del Norte. He stopped boarding with him because the Mexican dishes were "too highly seasoned with *chili colorado*." *Journal*, p. 315.

38. Leandro Gómez was the owner of a gristmill in El Paso del Norte. Gibson had employed him to grind flour for his company on the way south. *Ibid*.

39. In June, 1849, Ponce's Ranch became the property of Benjamin Franklin Coons, then prominent in the Santa Fe trade. In September of the same year the army established the Post of El Paso on the ranch. R. W. Frazer, *New Mexico in 1850: a Military View* (Norman, 1968), pp. 35–36.

40. Gibson's palmetto was the yucca, several species of which grow in the area. Josiah Gregg mentioned the *"palmilla*—a species of palmetto." *Commerce of the Prairies*, Max Moorhead, ed. (Norman, 1954), p. 113. Wislizenus wrote that the yucca resembled the palm tree "and therefore [was] commonly called palmilla." *Memoir of a Tour*, p. 25. The yucca is a member of the lily, not the palm family.

41. On the way south Gibson wrote that the water in the lagunita was so brackish "we could not even make coffee fit to drink." *Journal*, p. 310. Hughes called it a "small salt lake." *Doniphan's Expedition*, p. 268. Edwards downgraded it to a "salt pond." *A Campaign in New Mexico*, p. 89.

42. "Greaser" was a vulgarism used by some Anglos in reference to Mexicans. Similarly, Mexicans applied the term "gringo" to Anglos.

43. Guadalupe Miranda earlier had been secretary to the governor of the Department of New Mexico. In 1841 Governor Manuel Armijo granted to him and Carlos Beaubien the enormous tract later known as the Maxwell Land Grant. After the United States occupied New Mexico, Miranda settled in what would soon become Doña Ana County. In 1847 he purchased a merchant's license in Santa Fe. Sheriff and Collectors Record of Collection of Revenue—Licenses,

1847–1867. New Mexico State Archives, Santa Fe. Miranda later rejected United States citizenship and moved to Chihuahua where he held various state government positions.

44. It is not clear whether this is Socorro, New Mexico, or Socorro del Sur, but it seems more probable that it would be the latter.

45. Doña Ana had only been in existence for a few years, which may account for Gibson's favorable opinion of its appearance.

46. Robledo, sometimes spelled Roblero, was a camping place at the southern end of the Jornada del Muerto.

47. San Diego was a camping place on the Rio Grande near the present town of Rincon. It was on an alternate branch of the trail, one which added a few miles but shortened the distance without water. It was also the location of the San Diego crossing of the Rio Grande.

48. The "late troubles" were the Taos uprising and related events of January 1847. They are discussed in Ralph Emerson Twitchell, *The History of the Military Occupation of the Territory of New Mexico from 1846 to 1851 by the Government of the United States* (Denver, 1909), pp. 122–46.

49. Los Organos (Organ) Mountains are east of the Rio Grande. Las Animas Mountains have not been identified. The Copper Mine Mountains are the Pinos Altos Mountains. Lieutenant John G. Parke, in connection with the Pacific railway survey, listed the principal ranges west of the Rio Grande in this area as the Copper Mine Mountains, Picacho de los Mimbres, and the Burro Mountains. *Reports of Exploration and Surveys to Ascertain the Most Practicable and Economical Route for a Railroad,* 33 Cong., 2 Sess., House Exec. Doc. 91, II, 20.

50. Aleman was a camping place near the center of the Jornada and is a station of the same name on the Santa Fe Railway. Water was sometimes found there in pools following a rain.

51. The Laguna del Muerto was simply a sink which sometimes contained water after a rain but was more often dry.

52. The Ojo del Muerto was five miles west of the trail in the Caballo Mountains. Animals were sometimes driven to the spring for water when the Laguna del Muerto was dry but it added a difficult ten miles to the crossing and, moreover, the spring was frequently the haunt of Apaches.

53. Point of Rocks is a low eminence, also called El Perillo, between Aleman and Robledo. It appears as Point of Rocks on most contemporary maps. On his way south Gibson called it "the Perilla, an isolated mountain in the valley." *Journal,* p. 297.

54. Fra Cristobal was the camping place at the northern end of the Jornada.

55. San Pedro appears on maps of the 1840s and 1850s as Don Pedro but is listed in the census of 1850 as San Pedro. It is on the east side of the Rio Grande opposite the town of San Antonio.

56. Bosque Siete appears on contemporary maps, just above "Don Pedro," as Bosquecito, east of the Rio Grande opposite the town of San Antonio.

57. On contemporary maps Gibson's Caneda appears as Canas, a few miles above Bosquecito. James W. Abert called it Las Cañas. *Abert's New Mexico Report,* p. 121.

58. Probably Thomas Biggs, a native of Pennsylvania, who was listed in the 1850 census as a farmer residing in Valencia County. He and Hugh N. Smith later purchased part of the upper Pedro Armendáriz Grant. Biggs died in 1854.

59. The town of Placeres appears on contemporary maps on the east side of the Rio Grande a few miles below Albuquerque. However, Gibson's reference may be to the placer mining district in the Ortiz Mountains, the present Golden.

60. Captain Benjamin Moore, Captain Abraham R. Johnston, and 2nd Lt. Thomas C. Hammond, all of the First Regiment of Dragoons, were killed on December 6, 1846, in the Battle of San Pascual, California.

61. La Joya de Sevilleta now usually appears on maps as La Joya.

62. This is probably the James Powers of [James] Hartley and Powers, who maintained a store on the south side of the plaza in Santa Fe. Among other merchandise they offered for sale goods imported from Old Mexico, including wines and dried fruits from El Paso del Norte. *Santa Fe Republican,* October 9, 1847. The partnership was dissolved in January 1848, but the store continued to operate as Hartley and [Henry] Cuniffe.

63. 1st Lt. Vincent R. Van Valkenburg was killed in the battle at Taos Pueblo on February 4, 1847.

64. Peter R. Pratte was sheriff of Valencia County in 1847. Valencia County Records, Prefect Court Records, 1847–1848, New Mexico State Archives. Apparently he left New Mexico before the 1850 census was taken.

65. James H. Quinn, a native of Maryland and a lawyer by training came to New Mexico as a member of one of the volunteer companies in the Army of the West. He was circuit attorney for the southern district, which consisted of Bernalillo and Valencia counties, 1846–49. He had a store on the Taos plaza and later engaged in a variety of business enterprises and was prominent in New Mexico politics until his death on December 31, 1856. *Santa Fe Weekly Gazette,* January 10, 1857.

66. William Curtis Skinner, a native of Connecticut and a lawyer by profession, was active in New Mexico politics until he was killed in a fight in Albuquerque in 1851. He resided in Peralta. In 1847 he was clerk of the circuit court.

67. This may be the F. Robinson who, according to the 1850 census, was a native of New York and a merchant residing in San Marcial.

68. On contemporary maps the settlements shown along this route were Tijeras, San Antonio, and San Pedro, all of which still exist.

69. Richard Campbell began his mining operations shortly before the outbreak of the Mexican War. At this time he was working a mine at the New Placers in the Ortiz Mountains. A native of St. Louis, he married María Rosa Grijalva in Taos in 1828. Abert, *Abert's New Mexico Report,* pp. 51–53;

and Angélico Chávez, "New Names in New Mexico, 1820–1850," *El Palacio,* LXIV (September-October, 1957); 299.

70. Fort Marcy was the earthwork erected in 1846 on an elevation northeast of and overlooking the plaza of Santa Fe. Not until several years later was the name applied to the military facilities adjacent to the Palace of the Governors.

71. Governor Bent and Captain Burgwin were killed in the Taos uprising. Wilson, who had been sutler for Colonel Price's regiment in Santa Fe, died as a result of illness.

72. Despite Gibson's optimism the health of the troops in New Mexico remained poor for several years. A long list of volunteers had been discharged a month before Gibson's return because of physical inability to serve. Among the common causes were chronic nephritis, chronic hepatitis, phthisis, scrofula, chronic diarrhea, chronic rheumatism, scurvy, and general debility. O. No. 152, April 1, 1847, RG 94, OAG, Orders, Army in New Mexico. Later in the year there was an outbreak of remittant fever, diagnosed as typhoid. There were several cases of scurvy among the troops "but no return of last year's horrors is anticipated." Deaths in the army hospital averaged four a week, including both soldiers and teamsters. *Santa Fe Republican,* October 1, 1847.

# 2

## Santa Fe to Fort Leavenworth

When Gibson returned to Santa Fe the one-year term of enlistment for all of the volunteers serving in New Mexico was approaching expiration. During the next few months the volunteer units would be ordered back to Missouri to be mustered out; however, those officers and men who elected to remain in New Mexico were discharged before their companies departed. The withdrawal of the volunteers left only two undermanned companies of regular army dragoons as the occupying force until additional volunteers arrived from Missouri and Illinois. In August, to strengthen this obviously inadequate force, four mounted companies, made up of officers and men who had accepted discharges in New Mexico and volunteers from the government teamsters were mustered in as the Santa Fe Battalion. Robert Walker, formerly adjutant of the Second Missouri Mounted Volunteers, was elected major.[1] Com-

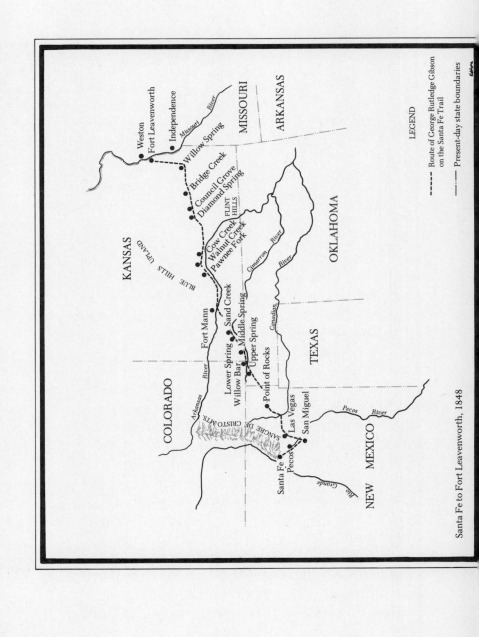

Santa Fe to Fort Leavenworth, 1848

LEGEND

------ Route of George Rutledge Gibson on the Santa Fe Trail

——— Present-day state boundaries

MISSOURI

ARKANSAS

KANSAS

OKLAHOMA

TEXAS

COLORADO

NEW MEXICO

Weston
Fort Leavenworth
Independence
Willow Spring
Bridge Creek
Council Grove
Diamond Spring
FLINT HILLS
Cow Creek
Walnut Creek
Pawnee Fork
BLUE HILLS UPLAND
Fort Mann
Sand Creek
Lower Spring
Willow Bar
Middle Spring
Upper Spring
Point of Rocks
Las Vegas
San Miguel
SANGRE DE CRISTO MTS.
Santa Fe
Pecos

Missouri River
Arkansas River
Cimarron River
Canadian River
Pecos River
Rio Grande

pany B, First Dragoons, which had been broken up in 1846, was reconstituted at this time, also with discharged volunteers.

Gibson was honorably discharged in Santa Fe but he was not among those who enlisted in the Santa Fe Battalion. Why Gibson, who had not seen his wife and young son for more than a year, decided to remain in New Mexico is unclear. Upon his arrival from Chihuahua he wrote, "I found there had been no mail since February and I determined to await the arrival of one, the state of things being such as to require it." Although he had kept his journal consistently since joining the volunteers he ceased to do so after the entry of May 5, 1847; hence, for the next year his day to day activities went unrecorded.

In September, 1847, the weekly *Santa Fe Republican,* the first American newspaper in New Mexico, began publication. It was printed in English and Spanish on a press imported by the army from St. Louis earlier in the year. The proprietors, Oliver P. Hovey and Edward T. Davies, both with some previous publishing experience, had come to New Mexico as members of the volunteer army and, like Gibson, had elected to remain in Santa Fe. They arranged with the chief quartermaster officer of the department to use the press to publish a newspaper and also printed a variety of materials for the army and civil authorities. The close relationship with the army is in-

dicated by the fact that the quartermaster assigned
Philip Gooch Ferguson, a private in the Third
Regiment of Missouri Mounted Volunteers, to
work in the printing office, for which he was
paid fifteen cents a day, the extra duty pay then
authorized by army regulations. After two weeks'
employment Ferguson departed when his company was transferred to El Paso del Norte.[2]

The first issue of the *Republican* appeared on
September 10, 1847. Gibson was employed to edit
it, but his name does not appear as editor until
the third issue, that of September 24. It is probably just coincidence that his announced association with the *Republican* coincided with Ferguson's
departure. More likely, his connection with the
newspaper dated from its inception, which might
account for his decision to be discharged in Santa
Fe. The *Republican* carried on its masthead the
inviting statement, "devoted to science, literature,
agriculture, the earliest news from the United
States and the general movements of the army,"
and added the somewhat extraneous sentiment,
"we die but never surrender." Under Gibson's
editorship it attempted to live up to the promise,
even though the latest news from the United
States was always weeks or months out of date
and the scientific and literary offerings were more
bucolic than instructive.

Local news was more fully covered, within the
limitations imposed by the four-page format and

the presentation of much of the material in both English and Spanish. Gibson, as editor, presumably had a free hand to express his opinion and make editorial comment, both of which freely interlarded the news items. One of them, often repeated, was praise of the improvements made in New Mexico, especially Santa Fe, since the beginning of the occupation. Equally noted were the improvements sure to come as "Anglo-Saxon Institutions and spirit . . . begin to show themselves in this interior and remote region." The "Savage Indians" who infested New Mexico would "speedily be subdued by the vigor of our arms" and the agricultural, pastoral, and mineral wealth of the province developed. By implication, at least, the Mexicans had neglected these resources, particularly mining, "so little understood and generally so badly managed."[3] Even so, for the most part Gibson was less critical of New Mexico and the New Mexicans in the columns of the *Republican* than on the pages of his journal. He also found it necessary to chide Americans for the erroneous opinions they had formed of New Mexico. Because the appearance of the country was "less attractive than their fancies had painted for them" and, he might have added, different from the well-watered East with which they were more familiar, they assumed it was worthless. In their ignorance they condemned such things as irrigation because they did not conform to practices in the States and, to the detriment of New Mexico, often expressed opinions without the knowledge to justify them.[4]

For the most part the *Republican* spoke highly of the army. As announced, army movements were regularly reported and efforts, no matter how futile, to deal with Indian depredations were praised. The officers, particularly Price, usually were mentioned in the most laudatory terms. On only one issue, military interference with the civil government, was the *Republican* strongly critical of military policy, and this may have reflected Gibson's legal background. Declaring that the citizens of New Mexico were "not aware that the laws framed and established by Gen. Kearney and confirmed by the President have been revoked," Gibson decried military arrogation of the powers of the civil courts. The people of New Mexico did not know where to turn "for just cause of complaint or the redress of any wrong," he charged, and legislative bodies, judges, and courts were meaningless if their acts could be overridden by the military authorities. "Why frame laws, if the order of a Commanding Officer is paramount?"[5] Col. Edward W. B. Newby, Fifth Illinois Volunteer Infantry, who commanded in New Mexico while Sterling Price was absent in the East, held essentially the same views. He, however, blamed the situation on failure to define the civil government sufficiently "to enable either the civil or military authorities to understand the exact extent of their powers." Hence, each frequently infringed, or was accused of infringing on the authority of the other, especially in matters of judicial jurisdiction.[6]

Gibson was aware of the problems facing the military and the civil government, their multifarious duties and conflicting interests. The situation was complicated by the distance from Washington and, in his opinion, the neglect of New Mexico by the Federal government. But, he also admitted the impossibility of issuing orders in Washington "suitable to the state of things and the country here." The *Republican* recommended that the public observe a sympathetic attitude toward the problems of the department commander.[7] It also praised Governor Donaciano Vigil,[8] calling him a zealous friend who had "taken a deep interest in the prosperity, welfare and improvement of New Mexico,"[9] thus lending its support to both civil and military authorities.

Gibson's career as a newspaper editor was equally as brief as his earlier ventures in publishing had been, lasting for about three months. The last issue published under his direction was that of December 18, 1847. The following week the *Republican* announced his resignation and expressed the hope that the paper would continue to exhibit the same "tact and ability" that Gibson had displayed.[10] Here again, Gibson's motives are obscure. Why he chose to terminate his employment when he did cannot be said. The *Republican* seemingly was doing well and certainly carried more advertising than any other New Mexican newspaper would for many years to come. It was not the time of year to cross the plains, for winter travel was both hazardous and uncomfortable. In fact, Gibson remained, presumably in Santa Fe, for another four months, doing what is not known as even the tenuous insight provided by his editorial comment is lost. It may be that the restlessness that characterized his entire career and led to frequent changes of residence and occupation contributed to the decision.

On April 28, 1848, when Gibson left Santa Fe to return to his home in Weston, he resumed his journal. He and his companions went first to Las Vegas where they were delayed for several days awaiting the arrival of the remaining members of their party. When the little group headed across the plains it consisted of only seven men. Gibson and Captain Anson Smith[11] were former officers in the Missouri volunteers and Major William Singer[12] was still on active duty. The other four, some of whom cannot be identified, presumably were civilians. The small size of the party was not especially unusual for the time, even though the route it took crossed an extensive area occupied by unsubdued Indians.

The Indians were not only unsubdued, they were actively hostile, taking advantage of the disorganization injected into movement along the Santa Fe Trail by the Mexican War. Inexperienced drivers, small trains and smaller groups of travelers, the involvement of the army in other areas all invited Indian depredations. It was estimated that in 1847 forty-seven Americans were killed, 330 wagons destroyed, and some 6,500 head of cattle taken by Indians along the Santa Fe Trail.[13] Most of these losses were suffered by government trains. This was by far the most serious assault on the trail since the beginning of the trade. Indian attacks were less frequent in 1848, but the prairie traveler was nonetheless aware of the menace.

The fact that the little party was entrusted with taking government mail to Fort Leavenworth is not surprising. The first contract to carry mail regularly between Missouri and New Mexico did not go into effect until July 1850. In the meantime the mail was carried in both directions by whatever means were available, sometimes by parties smaller than Gibson's.[14] In some cases individual contracts were made for carrying the mail, as, for example, in 1848, when a contract was made with J. M. Folger to carry the United States mail from Santa Fe to Fort Leavenworth and return for $600, the round trip to be made within seventy days.[15] If Gibson's party had a contract it has not been located and Gibson did not mention it.

En route to New Mexico the Army of the West had taken the mountain branch of the Santa Fe Trail. In returning to the States the Gibson party followed the shorter Cimarron branch. From Las Vegas, the easternmost settlement in New Mexico, to the recently established Fort Mann[16] on the Arkansas River, near the point where the two branches of the trail reunited, was almost 350 miles through country inhabited only by Indians. Beyond the fort it was more than 200 miles to Council Grove and, if not civilization, almost to home. Although wagon trains and travelers might pass over the trail at any time of year, most travel occurred between early May and late September when grass and climate were more favorable. War, with its unusual demand for military stores, was not a normal time, yet Gibson's party did not meet any westward bound trains until May 10, but from that date it encountered increasingly heavy traffic, carrying both private and government freight, far more than had moved over the trail in the prewar period.

Gibson's little party experienced many of the dangers and discomforts of travel across the plains and, indeed, expected that this would be the case. Waterless stretches and, at the other extreme, tremendous thunder storms accompanied by high winds, downpours, and flooding, shortage of grass with the consequent breakdown of animals, cold meals, hastily prepared meals, or no meals at all, nights spent in travel and nights spent huddled under wet blankets, encounters with Indians, always with the fear that they might prove hostile, accidents with firearms, all of these were normal aspects of the prairie crossing and Gibson and his companions escaped none of them. There was also the inevitable buffalo hunt. Only one animal was killed, a calf, but others were wounded and left to live or die as fate decreed. In a sense this segment of Gibson's journal recounts a familiar story, though one with infinite variations.

Gibson's journal leaves several questions unanswered. It is obvious that Gibson did not like Singer, though why he does not disclose, and since it was Singer who went ahead, leaving Gibson to follow, it would seem that the dislike was mutual. Whatever the cause, it must have been fairly serious to induce the already small party to split up as it did in the heart of the Indian country. Who, specifically, was entrusted with the mail is not clear, but apparently it was not Major Singer; at least, it was Gibson's portion of the party, reduced to only two men by the end of the trip, that delivered it at Fort Leavenworth. Of the two Anson Smith is the more probable candidate, for a month later he headed back over the trail with the mail for Santa Fe. This time he made the trip in nineteen days, thought to be "the quickest trip ever made by any person who has had charge of a mail."[17]

The following and final section of the journey carries the title "Journal of a Return Trip from Santa Fé to Fort Leavenworth in the Spring of 1848 with the United States Mail."

*Friday April 28h [1848]*

Against all prognostications and after saluting our friends with a parting benediction we left Santa Fe after a two years residence in Mexico, heartily glad that our faces were once more turned homewards and our backs to the rough adobie walls of the Country. Of course we had a thousand messages and a thousand little requests, from those we left behind, all having something of a Public or private nature to communicate. Several of our acquaintences bound for the Navijo Country escorted us out some miles and all went on well until we crossed the Arroyo Hondo our mules being so far tracticable and gentle. Here however the best and most spirited, by the bad arrangement of a Pack, part of which tumbled off, took a notion to use its heels for drumsticks and thus put the Devil in one which Capt. Smith rode, and he commenced charging up and down the arroyo to our great amusement. For a while all was well, but the breaking of one of Uncle Sams straps caused the mule to go one way and the rider the other, to his discomfort and to our great mortification and annoyance, where we were delayed some time hunting up the refractory animals. All being again made ready, we went on with out much further interruption and camped at the mouth of the Cañon, where a Mexican joined and camped with us on his way to San Miguel.[18] Our camp is 18 miles from Santa Fe and is a deep Cañon or pass in the mountains with barely room for a road and steep perpendicular or overhanging cliffs on each side, presenting some pretty scenery of a very wild character.

*Saturday April 29h*

After a cup of coffee we packed up, the morning cloudy, chilly and damp and ascended the mountains until they were on both sides of us enveloped in clouds and mists and the weather by no means warm. It rained, snowed or misted all day, and the highest summits of the mountains were perfectly white with snow. The afternoon especially was quite a winter day, but our great coats and blankets kept us comfortable. We passed old Pecos, the last relict of the Montezumas in this region;[19] the work and proud monument for many centuries of a race now extinct, and in the evening reached San Miguel, about 28 miles, where we took quarters at the house of our late guest, Don Lucian Trujillo, who treated us with the greatest attention and respect, being Alguazil [sheriff] of the County. We found the [Pecos] River high, but not enough so to impede our course, and we had an invitation to a Fandango got up on account of our arrival, but prefering rest, retired after supper to our blankets and enjoyed a pleasant sleep.

*30th*

The good accommodations prepared us for an early start, the day warm and pleasant, and we had nothing of interest, passing through the miserable Town of Tuckelota [Tecolote] and early in the evening came to the valley of Las Vegas, the last place we have a chance to procure any thing and where you see the great plains which extend to the states. It [Las Vegas] is a poor place garrisoned by two companies under command of Maj. [Israel B.] Donaldson[20] and we expect to be delayed here several days. We will adjust every thing here for our long march and when we leave bid Fare well to Civilization for one month. We were quartered in the Hospital for the want of a better place and our mules picketed.

*Monday May 1st*

Being delayed here several days we find it difficult to amuse ourselves or to pass the time with either pleasure or comfort so miserable is the place. Of all things keep me from a Mexican Frontier Town without the least thing to amuse or interest you, or without any way to spend your time. There was a Fandango last night (Sunday) got up they said for us, but none of us went, and to day there was a wedding, the happy pair (of the unshaved and unwashed class) marching through Town escorted by rude music and a fiew dirty men, women and children, some of whom continued as fast as they could to fire off old fashioned muskets every fiew minutes until they reached Home. Amongst the fiew animals of the country between which and our I see no perceptible difference I may mention the Dove, Blackbird, Crow, Robin and Blue Bird. The Rabbit of the U.S. can perhaps also be found here in some parts, but all animals as a general thing are different.

*May 2d*

After seeing that our mules were well fed, as we have to await for orders from Santa Fe, two of the Company visited the upper Town and Capt. Smith and myself went a fishing. One party brought in two chickens and some eggs and the other Fish so we have something more to eat than Bacon and hard bread.

A most unfortunate accident occurred this evening to Mr. Mace, one of our Company. He went to untie his mule and stooping down his pistol fell out of his belt and struck a log and went off shooting him about 2 inches above the stomach. He is still alive though we have but little hopes of his recovery. It was extracted from the right side of his back bone. He is an excellent man and it was much regreted by all.

*Wednesday May 3d*

Mr. Mace is still alive and we have hopes of his Recovery but chances are against him.[21] Maj. Singer arrived today and we leave tomorrow. He brings news that Genl. Price is ordered back to New Mexico by [Major] General [William O.] But-ler[22] and that the Treaty negotiated had been confirmed by the U.S. senate with slight modifications. Capt. Smith killed today 2 ducks and a prarie Dog all of which we cooked and eat *"con mucho gusto."*

*May 4h*

All things being ready, we left the last settlement to try once more the great plains, as well provided with mules and necessary things as the country would admit of. Our party consists of Smith and myself and two men, Maj. Singer, Servant and Teamster, in all 7 well armed and in fine spirits. Swift[23] has a musket, Raymond[24] my carbine and Smith and myself Halls Patent Rifles. We took

30 days rations of Hard Bread
30 days rations of Coffee
30 days rations of Sugar
30 days rations of Salt
30 lbs of Bacon

*and had 5 mules*

1 for myself
1 for Smith
1 for Raymond
2 for pack animals[25]

We passed the Mora [River] and camped on a little stream [Wolf Creek] 4 miles this side, where we killed 2 ducks. Antelope were to be seen all day in abundance but we never stopped to shoot any. The weather was windy and disagreeable, blowing almost a constant gale from the mountains but we travelled 25 miles, and had plenty of wood, water and grass.

*Friday May 5h*
After an early breakfast we left camp, having Antelope throughout the day in great abundance, but never stopped to hunt. Capt. Smith thought he saw Indians and being now in the dangerous country it made all more cautious and kept our little party on a constant look out. The game of all kinds appeared alarmed as far as we could see, which confirmed our impressions that Indians were near. We travelled as fast as possible to get

out of their reach and in the Evening at dark camped on the Ocaté [Creek], 38 miles, where we had grass and water but no wood.

## May 6h

As usual we left at 6 oclock and only stopped at the Rio Colorado[26] to lay in a supply of water, having it only at long distances for 500 miles. Early in the Evening we stopped and watered our mules at the Point of Rocks and then continued our march 5 miles further and encamped, having seen smoke both above and below us on Red River and other indications of Indians being in the neighbourhood, with whom we have no particular desire to form an acquaintance, as they are Camanches or Apaches or both. We have only a little brush at camp, scarcely sufficient to boil Coffee, but the grass is passible and there is water in a Ravine. We travelled to day 30 miles.

## May 7h

The Mountains have all disappeared except a fiew detached spurs, extending at long intervals into the prarie, all of volcanic origen. Maj. Singer's shot gun went off as he threw it into the wagon today but fortunately did no damage except to blow to pieces a musket. We made a long days march and camped at Rabbit Ear with a little wood and plenty of water at Whetstone [Creek] the other side.

*Monday May 8h*

We travelled 20 miles to day and found no water and had to continue 17 further before we could, both ourselves and our animals suffering very much. Every thing goes wrong and the pronostications about us leaving on Friday seem to be verified. My mule gave out to day and with great difficulty I got it to McNees creek where we nooned it, but found no water for them, the creek being dry. The weather is pleasant but windy with fleecy clouds indicating that some change was brewing or that we were approaching a different climate. The young grass is coming up and we begin to look for Buffalo.

Prarie Woodcock. This is a common bird on the plains and is said to be good to eat. They have a peculiar whistle which at night sounds like the scream of a bird of Prey and is often heard at all hours when you are standing as centinel and serves to dispel drowsiness by its wildness and keenness.

We camped off the road on Cedar Spring, with wood and water but no grass, all tired and happy once more when we could quench our thirst. Our mules are failing fast having almost had nothing to eat for the past 3 days and we begin too feel anxious lest we are put afoot.

We saw more sign of Indians but have had the good luck not to meet any of the Red faced Rascals.

A heavy cloud hung all evening in the North

and we were threatened with rain, but it passed by, giving us only a cold and strong wind.

We reached camp at Sundown after travelling over a barren country, destitute of all things, for 32 miles.

*Tuesday May 9th*

The morning was cold, cloudy, and damp, more like winter than summer and both ourselves and our animals suffered, the one from cold and the other from hunger and cold. Yesterday and today we passed over one continuous plain apparantly extending from McNees Creek to the Cold Spring, and generally the vision was not bounded by a single elevation, tree or shrub, nothing but one continued flat, the extent of which the eye could often not reach in any direction. We saw in the distance either Buffalo or Indians, signs of the last we saw in several places. After a march of 14 miles we stopped and nooned it at the Cold Spring, one of the fiew pretty places on the road with good water and plenty of grass. The spring gushes out from under a ledge of rocks, cold, clear and refreshing to the traveler. Smith here killed a rabbit and Maj. Singer 6 snipe so we once more have fresh meat. The weather is windy, cloudy and very cold for the season. We continued our march and in 5 miles came to the Cimmarron Bluffs,[27] composed of sand stone, and continued down parallel to the River about 12 miles where we descended in to the bottom and camped on the Bank with an abundance of grass of a good quality for the first time. Our mules eat it greedily and soon filled themselves after having empty stomachs for several days or nearly so. The stream itself is generally small, and the bottoms extensive, covered with verdure something like our praries, but with all their fertility presents a singular appearance as not a stick of timber is to be seen and the hills are quite barren and desolate. The water is good. No one would suspect the upper spring to be where you cross the bed of a dry creek. They say there is nothing in names, but in this instance all find there is.

The whole country is prarie, not a stick of timber, or plant or shrub to be seen except those usually found on Praries. Ducks, Geese, Crane, etc are common and the valley is enlivened by the songs of more than one species of the American Songsters, Robins, Larks, Blackbirds etc in abundance to which we have been almost entire strangers for 2 long years. In fact the valley bears in this respect some resemblance to the U.S. and has an interesting appearance to men who have been so long in a country where nothing but the naked ground could be seen.

*May 10th*

We made an early start, the road leading down the valley and we found it very sandy. In 6 miles we reached the Willow Bar which is nothing but a bank 3 feet high, with water occasionally in a Pool, and not a single willow to be seen, if ever any grew there. A short distance this side we passed a formidable row of 92 mule heads placed in double line which Mr. Spirer[28] lost in one night in 1844 in a snow storm, frozen to death. The grass down the bottom is fine and the road deep sand, but our mules get along well, having plenty to eat. In 12 miles we stopped to noon it and lunched. After a further march of 8 miles we had an alarm and flints were screwed in, pans primed and all things made ready for a fight. Proceeding on we went but a short distance before we discovered a train of wagons in the distance and knew relief and help were comeing if attacked. Continuing on, in 2 miles we came to a train of 30 wagons belonging to Lightner, Herd, and Shaw,[29] when salutations were exchanged and a thousand inquiries made. We learned from them that a large Band of Kiawas had passed from the Arkansas across the Cimarron near Sand Creek a fiew days before on their way to the lower Arkansas, that nothing had been heard from Gilpin[30] and that we probably would not see an Indian, about which I have doubts. I gave them the last number of the Republican as containing all the news. They had an Escort of 20 men under command of a Lieutenant, who were anxious to return with us, but we had no means of transportation and they were compelled to go on. The train also had a piece of Artillery and stood in no need of an escort. This meeting on the Plains always leaves one in good spirits as you get news from the road and furnishes something for the mind to dwell on whilst wandering over solitudes scarcely relieved by the hum of an insect and such we now found the case. We were sorry the Troops could not turn back with us, and after gathering all the news came on 7 or 8 miles and camped.

Capt. Smith killed 3 Geese today and we have an abundance of fresh meat and will fare well tonight and tomorrow.

The Evening is the first very pleasant one we have had and we enjoyed it, smoking and reposing on the ground, as the sun shed his silvery and mild light over us and then dropped in the western Horizon.

After we had retired to our Blankets Mr. James Elliot[31] and another person rode into camp bringing us news from the U.S. as late as the 16th of April. They had nothing of consequence and repeated the news that we would not probably meet Indians and then went on to join the trains ahead and we went to our Blankets to ponder on the events of the day, the news, our prospects etc.

*Thursday May 11h*

In the morning soon after starting we met Mr. Reed's[32] train accompanied by an Escort of 19 men, who were trying to overtake the one ahead. After travelling about 20 miles and suffering for

water and our mules weak for the want of sufficient provender we stopped to noon it and Maj.
Singer went on *new con* [sic]. We waited several
hours to recruit our animals, which had been
much worsted, and then left for Sand Creek
which we supposed to be about 24 miles distant
and where we expected to encamp for the night.
The day was the warmest we have had, and both
ourselves and animals suffered for water in the
afternoon when we left the road, which passes
over the high ground butting up against the valley, and took a near cut to the [Cimarron] River
where we procured water for ourselves by digging out a place in the sand, where some Fellow
Traveller had preceded us. They [the mules] had
plenty of grass though once more which helped
them much. The surface of the River bed is perfectly dry, but water can always be procured by
digging two or three feet in the sand with your
hands and *we* found it good. Even fish it is said
are sometimes found comeing out of the sand
with the water. It is curious to find water at least
so near the surface and furnishes a subject for
much remark to Travellers. The River appears to
be a great chasm or Cañon filled with sand,
through which it runs, the subterranean vents
being often filled up, by some unknown cause
and producing an overflow on the surface by the
obstruction it meets with. Some suggest volcanic
action for this peculiarity in the stream, but the

first appears to be the better theory. The valley or bottoms are rich and covered thick with good grass.

We saw a stray Buffalo today, the first we have seen to know it. Maj. Singer was by no means a pleasant companion to travel with, and but for the strength his party gave us [we] should have abandoned him long ago, as we would much rather be without him.

The water in the middle spring is good genuine spring water and in abundance; we passed it a fiew miles after leaving camp this morning.

We have passed over a succession of ridges today except a stretch of about 15 miles which presented the most beautiful specimen of the *Mirage* my eyes ever beheld. We appear to be surrounded by a spring flood, overflowing the green prarie, and the reflection of objects in the distance could be as distinctly seen as in the clearest mountain Lake under the sun.

The River has no banks and generally you would not suppose it the bed of a stream.

In the Evening we had a fatigueing march and never stopped until after night, when we again decended to the River by the Road and found ourselves 10 miles above the Lower Spring instead of at it, and at least 18 short of the place we expected to reach. The natural inference was that instead of 36 it is near 46 miles from the Middle to the Lower Spring.[33] We found Maj. Singer encamped here, unable to get further and we had tolerable grass and water, both of which were much needed.

*Friday May 12th*

We were on the road early and after 10 miles travel stopped at the Lower Spring to rest our animals and let them grase, where we found plenty of water in a large spring and good grass all around.

Just after leaving camp we passed an Indian trail which appeared fresh enough to have been made yesterday, and must have been made since the trains we met passed along. As it was a large one and probably of hostile Indians, we considered ourselves fortunate in not being a day sooner, for in that case we should have met and probably have lost our scalps.

The weather continued warm and pleasant and we have a long stretch between this and the Arkansas [River] without wood, water or grass. If we pass through this dreary waste safe, I shall begin to think all will go well with us, take the trip altogether, for we can then be better supplied with what our necessities call for.

Around and for several miles above the lower Spring the bottoms contract and it wears the appearance of a River with banks.

We saw several Buffalo straglers from the great herds which roam the plains. They generally are found in abundance in this section, but at present range farther East. We stopped and nooned it at Sand Creek and let our mules pick from the scanty grass all they could and get a good rest before we cross the plains to the Arkansas. At 3 oclock we were upon the road expecting to travel day and night, with 4 canteens of water our whole supply for 60 miles. We stopped a short time after travelling 12 miles just before night, and eat some cold bread and meat and grased our mules on the short buffalo grass.

After travelling at night 8 miles further I was compelled to stop from indisposition, being unable to do so [travel] from exhaustion, lost of rest for several nights, the want of water and hot weather. In about an hour we caught up and I made out to get 8 miles further on our road when I was forced to stop again from the same cause where we unsaddled and concluded to wait for morning and sleep a little. Day light found us in bed and then sun up, when we discovered 2 buffalo near us and Smith went and shot several times at one wounding it badly, but unable to get it. We then started considerably refreshed by the rest, but suffering for water and proceeded on


## The 13th May

To the Battle ground,[34] finding Buffalo in numbers all along the road. Near this place we distinctly hear a gun near us in some ravines and all were on the *qui vive* expecting to meet Indians every moment, Maj. Singer being ahead, having passed on in the Evening when we stopped to eat and rest. We proceeded on 2 or 3 miles when we came to a herd of 60 Indian horses grazing by the road side, and then fully expected trouble. We hurried on all our jaded animals possibly could, hoping to get out of their neighbourhood before discovered. All was expectation, anxiety and attention but we could still see the track of the Maj. waggon and concluded that the danger was ahead. Before we had traveled far we espied some men on an elevation ahead and when we approached distinguished them to be the Maj., who evidently were in trouble and rejoicing at our approach. Coming up, they told us they had been driven from their wagons after being surrounded by a large party, that they had looked with much anxiety for us, and that they fled to save their scalps. We could see a body of men watching our movements from a sand Hill on the Arkansas near the crossing and after proceeding a short distance on our way saw them descend and approach towards us. When they came near enough we discovered there were only 3 Indians with an old piece of blanket for a flag, having nothing else to use, and we met them and talked some time by signs and in Spanish, enough of which they had picked up to make themselves intelligible. They told us they were Kiowas hunting buffalo and were athletic, robust and warlike in their appearance and very well mounted, armed with bows and arrows which they said was all the arms they had. They were perfectly naked and neither used bridles or saddles, and their every action was that of the Lords of the Plains. We smoked and made them presents and they laughed at the Maj. and his party running and seemed to know them. They said all the Indians between us and the River were Kiawas and that there were a great many; that the guns we heard were a band of Camanches with them also hunting buffalo and that there camp was on the River where we saw smoke (probably 10 or 15 miles distant). After promising us friendship and telling us the Comanches were hostile we shook hands and parted, they for their camp, we to get out of the neighbourhood as fast as possible. We were still not in sight of the Maj. waggon but in a short time it came to our view, distant a mile or two in a sort of valley between the 1st range of sand hills and second, the Maj. having told us it was concealed in a hollow so that he had hopes they would not find it.

Long before we came to the wagon it was in our view, stripped of every thing, even the cover, and every thing which had value in their eyes being carried off. His trunk was broken open, his mules and valuables gone, even his sword and uniform and many of his papers.[35] We picked up some bacon and a fiew crackers, enough to last us to Manns Fort, and attempted to go on but, just as we started, the pack mule having our provisions stampeded, scattering every thing over the plains, so that our troubles were greatly augmented and a short allowance of provisions stares us in the face. After trying ineffectually to catch the mule, which no doubt smelt the Indians, and ran off and joined the herd of Indian horses, we went on, leaving every thing pretty much as we found it. We were suffering for water and traveled with all speed to the River, expecting an attack there from a large body of Indians, as none were to be seen on the road, but on our approach we only saw a stragler or two on this side. After watering our animals we came on, the neighbourhood being very unsafe for a small party as the Camanches with the Kiawas are hostile, and were immediately above us on the River. We continued travelling until 9 oclock at night and then stopped, built camp fires and laid down to take some rest and let our animals grase, both of which were much needed by our long and arduous marching. At 12 oclock we started again and traveled until day light when we were compelled to stop by the exhausted state of Maj. Singer, within about 7 miles of the Fort. We walked turn about and the day was very warm and in consequence our mules and ourselves were used up.

*Sunday May 14h*

After a cup of Tea the Maj. was able to travel on and we soon came in sight of the Fort and a large train of wagons just leaving camp. The Indians on yesterday could have mustered no doubt several hundred.

We were kindly received by the commandant, Capt. [William] Peltzer,[36] who administered to all our wants, and quartered us in the shantie occupied by himself, which scarcely furnished protection against the weather, but of course was the best they had, the whole having been constructed in the greatest haste and with a very limited supply of materials. After a siesta which refreshed us, we spent the remainder of the day in preparing to move forward.

Capt. Peltzer fitted out an expedition against the Indians, which proved abortive and they returned the same evening, the Capt. reporting he had seen a large body of Indians near our last camp when he was separated from his men, which if true shews the Camanches had followed us to that place. The Capt. gave us an order on the Quarter Master for a pack saddle and other things and Mr. Raymond having taken passage in a wagon train returning from this place to the states, we shall move forward tomorrow. Maj. Singer also procured mules and provisions and continues his journey.

*May 15h*

As soon as we could catch up we bid fare well to our hospitable friends and hurried on to join a train of 32 wagons and several discharged soldiers which left yesterday, for the States, the Pawnee and Osage Indians, being on the road between this and the big bend of the Arkansas and rendering travelling dangerous for a small party.

Mann's Fort (so called after the builder) is only temporary sheds of the rudest kind, and is situated in the low, flat bottom of the Arkansas, about 100 yards from the River, and 25 miles below the crossing.

In the afternoon whilst we were on the Road a severe thunder storm came up, and we were all well drenched, and found but little comfort with the train when we overtook it, having to lay down and sleep in our wet blankets. Wood also was not to be had and wet and chilly we spent an uncomfortable night 25 miles from the Fort.

We kept the mail dry with my Buffalo robe and the flour with a cougar skin brought from Santa Fe for the purpose, but every thing else was wet.


*May 16h*

The morning was cloudy and damp but indicative of fair weather, and we all set off. The train had a large lot of loose cattle which they were taking back to the states and this with other things we expect to produce delays. We travel from early in the morning until about 2 oclock when we turn out and grase the balance of the day, the grass being abundant and good in the River bottom. This furnishes rest both to ourselves and our animals which we much need. In the Evening the sun came out and by spreading our blankets dried them, so that we can have another comfortable nights rest.

Our camp is in a pretty bottom of the River, and we picked up drift wood enough to answer all purposes and fare for the day tolerably well.

*Wednesday May 17h*

We have in company a strange customer, no other than a woman in mans clothes.[37] She enlisted in Col. Gilpins Batallion and performed all her duties as a soldier, nor was her sex suspected until she disclosed it herself. There is nothing in her appearance suspicious and she mixes with the Teamsters as one of them, and smokes, chews and acts the man. Her sex being discovered she was sent back to the States by this train and furnishes rough jokes daily for these men of hardy habits. She has not yet laid aside mans clothes.

We got under way early, the morning clear and warm, and traveled steadily until we camped on Coon Creek. Some of the company said they saw Indians but if they did, they were in small numbers, and as yet have not molested us or approached close.

We have from necessity been compeled to use the "*Bois de vache*" for fuel since we first struck the Cimmorron, and it is a good substitute for wood in dry weather, but very poor in wet.

There was a heavy dew last night, indicating a different climate from that in which we have been.

*May 18h*
Early in the morning we were under way and about noon arrived at the Pawnee Fork, seeing fresh Indian sign, but no Indians. No Buffalo were here having been no doubt driven away by the Indians. After a little delay in crossing (the banks being high and steep) we all found ourselves safely on this side, and came on the Ash Creek which was perfectly dry. As we could not camp there we came 10 miles further, turning off the Road to the River for water, near which we camped on the Bank of the Lone Elm [Creek] with good grass and an abundance of fine clear water.

Swift shot a coon at camp and we tried to get some Buffalo which could be seen on the River but failed.

The Evening was cloudy with Thunder showers in all directions, and we enjoyed it, reposing upon the green sward near the water.

Our days travel was about 28 miles and it sprinkled rain a little in the evening.

*May 19h*
The morning was clear and pleasant and a fiew miles from camp we came upon a large Herd of Buffalo, directly upon our road. Girths were at

once tightened, guns and pistols examined, and every thing dispensed with that could encumber or impede in a long chase, it being determined to adopt that method of hunting. Before we came near them the whole body set forward with that awkward looking and rolling motion so peculiar to this animal, when 4 horsemen went in pursuit, mounted upon large and well made American horses in the best order. We all stopped to look on, having a full view of the whole country in all directions. Soon they come up with them, you hear a report of arms, see the flash and the herd separate before the horse and rider, you hear another and another, but in the meantime horsemen and buffalo are lost to your view. They soon however come in sight again, but instead of the herd they pursue some cows and calves which they singled out as the best and which they turned, so as to bring them directly to us. When they come near enough the men ran out from the wagons to shoot them, but could not fire on account of the close proximity of the horsemen and we felt sure we should have plenty of meat. But the obstinate animals kept on to the River, disappearing in the sand hills, and the horsemen were soon seen returning in pursuit of a calf, which ran almost up to the train, and was only killed after great exertions and by the assistance of a dog belonging to some of the company. It had been shot in the throat early in the chase, yet run probably 10 miles before it was captured. A cow also had been shot and fell, but got up and ran off faster than ever. One of the horsmen persued another calf to the River, but loosing his powder horn could not kill it and had to return with his lips down. It is astonishing how tenacious of life this animal is, nothing but the most deadly shot enabling the hunter to get his game. Nothing like hunting or amusement, in America at least, will compare with a Buffalo chase in excitement and interest where several go out well mounted and well prepared. It takes more than a common horse to overtake them and some refuse (as one did today) to run close up to them, in which event you of course are disappointed. The day was very warm, the sun being disagreeably hot, and we turned off the road and camped on the River 5 miles from Walnut Creek, with wood, water and grass plenty.

We tried fishing in the River and failing to get a bite gave it up as a bad job.

We herd [sic] and saw partridges to day and the nights bring heavy dews, an evidence, if we had nothing else, that we were in a different climate from that of New Mexico.

In the afternoon and evening we baked bread, having lost all by the stampede of our mule above the crossing of the Arkansas and there being only flour at Manns Fort. The only cooking utensils we have are a frying Pan and Coffee Pot, so we take advantage of the opportunity and borrow from the Teamsters. Sometimes we make *Slap-jacks,* flour thickened with water and a little salt, and fry cakes similar to Buck wheat in the grease of bacon.

### Saturday May 20h

The morning was cool and bracing and before we left camp we could see a Train En route between us and Walnut Creek which proved to be Copeland and McShane[38] and others and just as we reached Walnut discovered another on the bank, Darton, Roberts[39] and others. As we reached the Big bend of the Arkansas we could see a large train corraled, which turned out to be Todd and Mayer, Bean and Masservy, McKnight and White,[40] and learned the road was strung with trains to the States. We took dinner with Bean and Masservy and had to carry a little more spirits in our hold than we have been wont; all of which we were likely to need, as a heavy cloud hung in the West.

The day being good to travel we stopped but a short time and came on to Cow Creek, nearly 30 miles and scarcely had time to camp, before the rain came upon us. Our baggage was in the wagons and the Captain of the train (Horner)[41] loaned us a Tent which we made out to get up and thus kept dry, but had to go without supper.

We found the Creek very high, past fording and unless we can construct a raft shall be compelled to wait until the waters subside, as the rain of this evening must raise it still higher. If detained here it will be for some time, but we have hopes of being able to cross Tomorrow.

Our fare was by no means agreeable but necessity makes men bear many things with a good grace, when all hope of relief is gone.

Our animals fared but little better than ourselves, as grass was very scarce and indifferent, but Capt. Horner gave us some corn which benefitted them much.

*Sunday May 21t*

The morning was fair and pleasant, and a warm cup of coffee prepared us for another days work, the difficulty being to procure materials to construct a raft as Cow Creek was impassible otherwise. Go forward, we must, somehow, being pretty well through the dangerous country, and where we can have wood, water, and grass plenty. After an Examination a Tree was found, which we could cut across the Creek. Capt. Smith accordingly swam over, with an ax, and cut it down, when we carried our packs across, and then swam our mules over at the road, thus crossing without further difficulty. We lost but little time packing up and were soon under way, finding the roads very muddy from the heavy rain last night. In 5 miles we came to Owl Creek and about 4 miles this side of that stopped and grased our animals, the grass good and Buffalo in abundance. We left Maj. Singer crossing and our party now consists of Smith, Swift and myself, enough as we will only meet friendly Indians if any atal.

Little Cow Creek is about 2 1/2 miles this side of the Big, and Owl Creek the same distance this side of that, but neither had water in them.

We are now evidently in a very different climate from the dry and elevated plains near Mexico, and you miss most of the plants peculiar to that region.

Two days more and we shall be at Council Grove, the Porta [sic] now of the great plains on this road.

We found Mr. Coons[42] in camp at the Little Arkansas but made no stay, having to travel by tomorrow 10 ocloc, 65 miles.

In 18 or 20 miles we came to one of the Turkey Creeks and stopped and eat a piece of bread at 10 oclock at night.

Whilst here Maj. Singer and party passed us and at 12 oclock we resumed our journey, travelling until just before day and passing Maj. Singer encamped at the Little Turkey Creek. We stopped and grased our animals and slept perhaps an hour, arriving at Cotton wood Fork at 10 oclock in the day. We met Mr. [blank] train in charge of Tom Boggs[43] about 7 miles from Cotton Wood and found on the Fork a part of J. Halls[44] train.

We found Buffalo in great abundance until we

crossed the Little Arkansas, when we left this huge animal of the plains entirely behind us.

We are all pretty tired and well worn out, and suffered last night for the want of water.

Just before day it sprinkled rain on us and after we started gave us quite a pretty little shower.

*May 22*

It is cloudy, very windy and rainy, though the last not hard. We were glad to reach camp and have a cup of warm coffee, having had nothing to eat since yesterday morning but a little bread. Where we shall be tonight will to a great extent depend upon the weather, having by no means such as suits travelling. We camped early at Cotton wood where we found a portion of Mr. Halls train awaiting the remainder, and after a Siesta and resting several hours, we resumed our journey and in the evening before sun down stopped at the Lost Spring.

The clouds seemed gathering from all quarters and the muttering thunder announced we were about to have rain, so we prepared for it, covering every thing with our skins and rapping ourselves up the best we could. There was no wood, nothing but the naked prarie, grass, water and a Bank which would serve to some extent to break the storm from us.

Every thing indicated a most violent one, clouds were flying in all directions, dark, heavy and threatening, and vivid flashes of lightning all around lit up the heavens and earth both with a fearful glare, so we determined to await it here, Maj. Singer and party passing on, just before it burst upon us. The rain came beating, not in gusts, but a general outpouring of the heavens, the low places sending down torrents and mother earth melted into a perfect quagmire. It can rain hard in the U.S. but fully to appreciate a severe storm let one be on the plains, where the wind meets with no obstruction and where shelter from the pitiless elements can not even be hoped for and one can realize the fruition of a comfortable house. Of course we fared badly and suffered both from wet and cold as it hailed enough to chill the atmosphere and continued to rain and blow until long after [mid]night, perhaps 2 oclock. As it came up we were trying to get something to eat but the rain soon extinguished our little fire and left us amongst other things with empty stomachs. The grass was good and our mules fared well but at one time were in danger from the torrents which came down the low grounds on which we had picketed them. High grounds, low grounds and all were water, and it was like a deluge. There we were, squatted down besides our packs, the rain beating, the wind blowing, the night hideously dark, and ourselves shivering, one of the many uncomfortable situations in which a traveller finds himself on these plains. After the storm, we made the best bed we could with our wet and dry blankets and laid down and slept soundly until morning, having had but one meal through the day.

*Wednesday* [Tuesday] May 23

The morning was cloudy with mist enough falling to wet us, but we were anxious to reach Council Grove and got off as soon as possible. It cleared off before we reached Diamond Spring and we stopped this side of it, cooked, dried our blankets and had a warm cup of coffee. We then came on to the Grove which we reached long before night, where we found Maj. Singer and party considerably worsted, having reached there a short time before us. We had bread enough cooked here to last us to the Fort after encamping in the Bottom on this side where the grass was best. We passed Howks[45] train at Diamond Spring and met Raymond[46] 5 miles this side, with whom we had a long talk and a glass of his best. His goods were freighted by a Mr. Brown.[47]

Council Grove has greatly changed in appearance since we went out and now presents a novel appearance to men from Mexico with its Log Cabins and Rail Fences and is an important point to

Travellers. Maj. Singer here procured a fresh mule but we could not and shall have to go on with our broken down and jaded animals. I met 2 men here, acquaintances from Weston, one of whom came out to camp to enquire about his son who belonged to my company and is now in the Santa Fe Batallion.

We looked with no little interest upon the hickory, oak and Walnut trees and never did I think them so beautiful as when spreading my blankets under the broad foliage of this gnarled favorite of the U.S.

Quite a laughible scene occurred to one of our pack animals today. He is blind of one eye and when we met Mr. Browns train was too busy watching it too see a deep sink hole near the road side, and all at once suddenly disappeared by stepping into it. There lay our mule and the mail, he flat of his back in a place not big enough for him to turn over, six feet deep and with straight perpendicular sides. We managed to get the mail off and then with the assistance of some men from the train lifted him on his feet, when he scrambled out and went to picking grass. We met J. Hall with a train just passing the Grove, but made no stop with him.

The evening was pleasant and several Kansas Indians came into camp, to one of whom we gave all of our spare coffee.

*May 24h*

We left camp in good season and came to the Big John [Spring] where we found several wagons and Mr. Beckam,[48] an acquaintance, with whom we took breakfast and smoked. As we left, they insisted upon us taking a cold shoulder of Bacon, well boiled, which we found very serviceable in the course of the day.

Before reaching the next stream,[49] 10 miles, it hailed and rained on us and the threatening appearance of the Heavens induced us to stop and camp, which we had barely time to do before a heavy storm of wind, Hail and rain came upon us and we determined not to leave camp until the weather was better. The old poles of an Indian Lodge enabled us soon to prepare a shelter and in a little while with our skins and blankets we were better prepared in the timber for a storm than we have been on the whole road.

The remainder of the day was stormy and the jaded condition of our animals made rest advantageous as other wise they might give out before we got to the Fort.

Bread and the cold bacon made our dinner and supper and we took in the afternoon a good sleep which refreshed us very much. The night was stormy, but we fared better than we expected in our wigwam, there being no one with us, Mr. Swift having gone on with Maj. Singer.

The grass the remainder of the road is good

and we expect to travel to suit the condition of our animals.

*May 25h*

We had every prospect in the morning of a good day so we packed up as speedily as possibly and took the road meeting Mr. Owens[50] train and then Doctor East[51] and Governor Hoffman[52] with each of whom we exchanged congratulations. We found the road heavy, and the day was sultry and warm so we get along slowly stopping to grase about noon. We met Beck[53] with Doctor East train and took a glass with him, which by no means hurt us or the great temperence cause.

Capt. Smith yesterday gathered a cup full of gooseberries and cooked them, but they were rather young to be good.

In the afternoon whilst our mules were grasing I caught some perch in one of the little streams we cross and in the evening had fish for supper. We camped early at the stream the other side of 110 [Mile Creek] with every thing in abundance, even musquitoes which annoyed us very much and disturbed our rest throughout the night. Here we saw the fire fly for the first time, heard a Great Owl hooting, with a forest which looks like home, our blankets being again spread under a broad oak, to keep off the heavy dews that fall at night. It was very warm and instead of sleep, Home with all its endearments and luxuries was passing through my mind and day light had like to have found me thinking of all that is near and dear to me. The nearer one approaches home after a long absence the more anxious he is to see it, and his feelings keep pace with his steps and most generally outrun them. Thus it is with me, anxious as I have been, to be there, my anxiety seems to be increased now when I draw comparatively near.

*May 26*
We made an early start and passed Ross and Irwins[54] train at 110 and Col. Davys[55] close behind and Waldo's[56] a fiew miles behind that and a Dutch train a fiew behind that. We also amongst those at the creek found a Government train. The rain day before yesterday extended all over this country and appears to have been equally heavy in all places. The day is pleasant, neither warm nor cold, dry nor wet and we stopped to noon it at Rock Creek. I feel sensibly the change from a dry to a damp climate, my skin not having that dry and scaly feeling it does in Mexico.
We meet great numbers of Kansas Indians who appear to have provisions packed on their animals. They all resemble each other and are far from being such looking men as the savages of the plains. In the afternoon we met a large Government train and come on to the Willow Spring

where we found another, and to our surprise a Log cabin and enclosure, with hogs, cattle and horses, the property of and inhabited by a Cherokee as we understood. Here we left the Independence road[57] and by dint of hard travelling reached Stone coal Creek, our mules barely able to make camp and ourselves considerably worsted.

We found the prarie in many places full of ripe strawberries, a great luxury to us, but we needed rest more and retired early to our blankets after gathering a fiew.

*Sunday* [Saturday] May 27h

We made an early start to cross the Kansas River, but lost our way and went down it, nooning at a pretty stream 14 miles from camp. We are threatened with more rain, and when we shall reach the Fort is now uncertain. We saw Mr. Hunter[58] of Westport who had been at the Pottawatamie payment with a party of 8 or 10 and they gave us directions how to take a near cut to our place of destination. Soon after leaving them, we stopped on a pretty stream, where we caught fish and having a squirrel made a hearty meal upon these two dishes. We traveled all day through the Delaware and Shawnee Country and saw many beautiful places, with neat cabins and good farms and fat horses, some of which looked remarkably well. We also saw a great many of the Indians, all neat and clean but with the taste peculiar to the race for flashy dress, deep colors and gewgaws and trinkets. We passed one house where a large party were assembled to dance, some of whom were pretty squaws. The country is rich and all the farms well cultivated, and presents much scenery which would vie with the most beautiful landscapes. The last 6 or 7 miles of our road, was over the bluffs by a trail, when we struck the Delaware Ferry,[59] where we found between 4 and 5 hundred head of fat cattle on their way to Santa Fe, and a train of wagons, some of which were crossing over and we were ferried across in a return boat. We also learned that troops were encamped on the road at Gum Spring, but as we did not follow the road [we] missed them. After passing through 6 miles of timber we camped two hours after night in the open prarie, pretty well tired out by a long days travel in very warm weather. We understand Maj. Singer got in on yesterday and we are now within 16 miles of the Fort. The Kansas [River] was full from the late rains, but we crossed without delay or difficulty.

*Monday* [Sunday] May 28h

We are sore and tired and our mules so given out that we could only travel 10 miles and stop and grase where the grass was good. The most of the time we were on foot, leading or driving as we are threatened with rain again.

At last the brick walls of the Fort loom up and here we are once more in the Fort, our mules broken down, the mail safely deposited in the office, ourselves entertaining our friends and acquaintences with the news and at the same time a hard shower watering mother earth. Of course we feel greatly relieved and I feel better satisfied, having found my trunk here, with many of my principal articles in it, but some missing. Rest we much need and I scarcely knew my own face, when I looked in a glass, not having shaved for nearly 40 days. But fiew of my acquaintences knew me at first, so metamorphised had I been by 30 days exposure on the plains, but home now I hope will bring me some comfort and rest and some of the very, real pleasures which mankind enjoy in this life.

Here ends 800 miles of travel by land over a country which almost is a Desert.

The steamer Whirlwind, Capt. Luke, goes down in the morning and will furnish a speedy conveyence to the place I most desire to see of all others, my own home and fireside.

Between the fifth and sixth sections of his journal Gibson inserted the following poem. Although there is nothing to indicate the time this was done, it seems probable that it was to commemorate his imminent departure for Missouri.

*The Welcome Back*
*By Eliza Cook*

Sweet is the hour that brings us home
    Where all will spring to meet us
Where hands are striving as we come
    To be the first to greet us
When the world hath spent its frowns and wrath
    And care been sorely pressing
Tis sweet to turn from our roving path
    And find a fireside blessing.
    Oh joyfully dear is the homeward track
    If we are but sure of a welcome back

What do we seak on a weary way
    Though lonly and benighted
If we know there are lips to chide and stay
    And eyes that will become love-lighted
What is the worth of the diamonds ray
    To the glance that flashes pleasure
When the words that welcome back betray
    We form a hearts chief treasure
    Oh joyfully dear is the homeward track
    If we are but sure of a welcome back

# Notes

## Chapter 2

1. Price to Roger Jones, July 20, 1847; and August 14, 1847, RG 94, OAG, Letters Received.
2. Philip Gooch Ferguson, "Diary, 1847–1848," in Ralph P. Bieber, ed., *Marching with the Army of the West* (Glendale, 1936), pp. 320–22.
3. September 10, 1847.
4. September 17, 1847.
5. October 30, 1847.
6. Newby to Jones, October 8, 1847, RG 94, OAG, Letters Received.
7. December 4, 1847.
8. Donaciano Vigil, born in Santa Fe in 1802, had played a role in the military and political life of New Mexico prior to the Mexican War. General Kearny appointed him secretary of the civil occupation government and he became acting governor when Governor Charles Bent was killed in January 1847. On December 17, 1847, Price, who was promoted to the rank of Brigadier General in July 1847, appointed Vigil "Civil Governor of the Territory of New Mexico." O. No. 10, RG 94, OAG, Orders, 9th Military Department. Vigil held office until Brevet Lieutenant Colonel John Macrae Washington arrived in Santa Fe in October 1848.
9. December 11, 1847; and December 18, 1847.
10. December 25, 1847. The *Santa Fe Republican* was published until 1849. The latest known existing issue is an

"extra" dated August 8 of that year. It is believed that the final issue was published about November 24, 1849. Pearce S. Grove, Becky J. Barnett, and Sandra J. Hansen, *New Mexico Newspapers* (Albuquerque, 1975), p. 480. The army sold the press at public auction on February 14, 1850.

11. Anson Smith was a captain in Willock's Battalion, Missouri Volunteers, part of the force that accompanied Colonel Sterling Price to New Mexico in 1846.

12. Major William Singer, Additional Paymaster, Volunteers, a native of Pennsylvania, was honorably discharged on March 4, 1849.

13. Henry P. Walker, *The Wagonmasters* (Norman, 1966), p. 261.

14. Morris F. Taylor, *First Mail West* (Albuquerque, 1971), pp. 13, 23–27.

15. Thomas L. Brent with J. W. Folger, December 20, 1848, RG 92, Records of the Office of the Quartermaster General, Register of Contracts.

16. Fort Mann was established in April 1847, on the Arkansas River west of the present Dodge City, Kansas. Crudely constructed of cottonwood logs, it provided some protection and facilities for repairs for trains passing along the trail. It was abandoned in 1850. Robert W. Frazer, *Forts of the West* (Norman, 1965), p. 56.

17. *Santa Fe Republican,* July 18, 1848.

18. San Miguel del Bado, probably established in 1795, was an important settlement on the Santa Fe Trail in the Mexican period. Today it is some three miles south of the Santa Fe-Las Vegas highway on the west side of the Pecos River, most of its adobe houses long since deserted. There has been some recent rehabilitation.

19. The ruins of Pecos Pueblo, abandoned in 1838 by the few descendants of its once large population, and Pecos mission church were often but wrongly attributed to the Aztecs by Americans who saw them in this period.

20. Major Israel B. Donaldson, Fifth Illinois Volunteer Infantry, was a Kentuckian by birth. He came to New Mexico with his regiment in the summer of 1847 and was hon-

*Notes*

orably discharged on October 16, 1848. See Lee Myers, "Illinois Volunteers in New Mexico, 1847–1848," *New Mexico Historical Review,* XLVII (January, 1972); 28. Troops were stationed in Las Vegas from time to time but the formal Post of Las Vegas was not established until October 2, 1849. The troops in Las Vegas were always quartered in rented facilities.

21. The *Santa Fe Republican* of May 31, 1848, reported, "Mase . . . died after two or three days of the most unparalled [sic] suffering from his wounds."

22. Major General William O. Butler, Volunteers, had replaced Major General Winfield Scott in command in Mexico City. Brigadier General Price was in the city of Chihuahua as a result of his unauthorized invasion of the state of Chihuahua.

23. Swift has not been identified.

24. Apparently there were at least two Raymonds in Santa Fe in 1848. Gibson's companion was probably William Raymond, a native of New York, who, in 1848, operated a dram shop. In 1849 he was co-proprietor of the United States Hotel in Santa Fe. He returned to Santa Fe sometime after June 24, 1848. Sheriff and Collectors Record of Revenue—Licenses, 1847–1867, New Mexico State Archives; and *Santa Fe Republican,* August 1, 1848.

25. These were the rations and animals for Gibson's portion of the party only. Major Singer had a wagon drawn by an unspecified number of mules and his own rations and equipment.

26. The Canadian River, which was also commonly referred to as the Colorado or Red river.

27. Cimarron Bluffs is not a usual place name on maps or in journals of the trail. Adolf Wislizenus wrote, "About five miles from the crossing [of the Cimarron], light bluffs rise in the prairie, consisting of yellow and reddish sandstone below, and a spotted sandstone, combined with lime and argyle, above." *Memoir of a Tour,* p. 14.

28. In a severe October snow and sleet storm in 1844 Albert Speyer lost many of the mules in his train near

103

Willow Bar. Edward J. Glasgow and Henry Connelly suffered almost equal losses in the same storm. Moorhead, *New Mexico's Royal Road*, pp. 89–90. Wislenzenus saw the bones of "about 100 mules" when he passed the spot in 1846. *Memoir of a Tour*, pp. 13–14.

29. H. Lightner, John Hurd, and Benjamin Shaw arrived in Santa Fe late in May. Lightner and Shaw left within a few days, taking all of their goods to Chihuahua. *Santa Fe Republican*, May 31, 1848. A merchant's license was issued in Santa Fe to "Heard and Co." Sheriff and Collectors Record.

30. Lieutenant Colonel William Gilpin, later the first governor of Colorado Territory, commanded a battalion of Missouri Volunteers, organized to control the plains Indians, particularly along the Santa Fe Trail. Thomas L. Karnes, *William Gilpin, Western Nationalist* (Austin, 1970), pp. 190–91.

31. James Elliot reached Santa Fe later in May and took out a license to engage in trade. *Santa Fe Republican*, May 24, 1848; and Sheriff and Collectors Record.

32. "Mr. Reid" and his train arrived in Santa Fe late in May. *Santa Fe Republican*, May 31, 1848.

33. Despite Gibson's skepticism the distance between the springs was usually given as about thirty-five miles. See Moorhead, *New Mexico's Royal Road*, p. 98.

34. The Battle Ground was the site of an engagement between small forces of Texans and New Mexicans on June 20, 1843. Barry, *Beginning of the West*, pp. 478–79.

35. James J. Webb, who arrived in Santa Fe early in June, reported that while his train was crossing the Arkansas River, "a large party of [Kiowa] Indians were seen coming up to them, but in a friendly manner, when the chief of the party informed them that a party of Americans, had left their wagon and mules—that they, (the Indians) were on a buffalo hunt—that they saw the Americans, and tried to give them signs that they were friendly Indians, but supposed that the Americans did not understand them—that the Indians had taken the mules from the wagon and everything in it, and had taken all to their camp except the

wagon, which they left where they found it. Mr. Webb ordered them to go and produce every article they had taken and deliver them over to him, which they did, with the exception of a cloak and some tobacco, as is supposed, and which was immediately sent to Mann's Fort." *Santa Fe Republican*, June 8, 1848.

36. William Pelzer of St. Louis, captain of the artillery company in Gilpin's battalion, was a German immigrant and apparently not too competent to deal with Indians or handle men. Karnes, *William Gilpin*, pp. 195–97; 202–3.

37. According to Gilpin's biographer, the young woman, Caroline Newcome, was enlisted as Private Bill Newcome. The deception was discovered when the private "became pregnant and went absent without leave." *Ibid.*, p. 196.

38. A. M. Copeland reached Santa Fe in June and rented the hostelry known as the Santa Fe House, renaming it the Independence House. *Santa Fe Republican*, July 24, 1848. Philip McShane was a Santa Fe merchant and dramshop proprietor.

39. Darton and Roberts have not been identified. W. T. Dalton was engaged in the Santa Fe trade at this time and for some years thereafter and Wilson Roberts held a license for a dramshop in Santa Fe in 1848. Sheriff and Collectors Record.

40. Henry Mayer, James C. Bean, William S. Messervy, James M. White, and William S. McKnight arrived in Santa Fe in July. (Todd has not been identified.) All except Bean, who probably took his goods on the Chihuahua, took out merchants licenses. *Ibid.*

Messervy, White, and McKnight played important roles of one kind or another in New Mexico's history. Messervy, a native of Massachusetts, migrated to St. Louis in 1834 and entered the Santa Fe trade in 1839. He had resided in Santa Fe for some years before he was appointed territorial secretary in 1853. In 1854 he was acting governor of the territory for four months.

White, who previously had been a merchant in Warsaw, Missouri, became engaged in the Santa Fe trade, probably in 1848. In October, 1849, he and the five male members of his party were killed by Jicarilla Apaches and Mohuache Utes near Point of Rocks on the Cimarron branch of the trail. The three female members were taken captive and none of them were recovered alive.

McKnight of St. Louis was a long-time Santa Fe trader. In 1849 he was appointed postmaster of Santa Fe. Though he later returned to St. Louis he continued to be active in the trade.

41. This was probably Edward B. Horner, who at this time was employed in hauling military freight in government trains between Fort Leavenworth and Santa Fe.

42. Benjamin Franklin Coons, a native of St. Louis, was prominent in the Santa Fe trade at this time. In 1849 he was one of the first settlers of what would later be El Paso, Texas, where he established a trading house and freighting business and also continued in the Santa Fe trade. A combination of unfortunate events and poor judgement led to Coons' bankruptcy in 1850. See Rex W. Strickland, "Six Who Came to El Paso: Pioneers of the 1840s," *Southwestern Studies*, I (Fall, 1963); 12–17.

43. Thomas O. Boggs was the son of Lilburn Boggs, one time governor of Missouri, and his second wife. As a young man Thomas was employed in the far-flung business enterprisesoftheBentsandSt.Vrain.DavidLavender,*Bent'sFort* (New York, 1954), p. 210. During the Mexican War he carried despatches for the army from New Mexico to both Fort Leavenworth and California.

44. Jacob Hall was associated with Dr. David Waldo, long prominent in the Santa Fe trade, in the firm of Waldo, Hall, and Company. They held the contract (in Waldo's name) for carrying the mail between Independence and Santa Fe from 1850 to 1854. With other partners Hall continued to hold the mail contract until 1860. See Taylor, *First Mail West*, chaps. 1–5.

45. Howk cannot be identified postively but is probably Solomon P. Houck of Boonville, Missouri, who had been in the Santa Fe trade since the 1820s and was one of the

traders who accompanied Doniphan's expedition to Chihuahua. He returned to Santa Fe from Chihuahua at about the same time Gibson did.

46. This probably was not the Raymond who had accompanied Gibson from Las Vegas and had gone on ahead with a wagon train from Fort Mann. *The Santa Fe Republican* of July 6, 1848, noted the recent arrival of M. Raymond from Missouri.

47. Probably James Brown, who in 1848 was the principal contractor for carrying military freight to Santa Fe. His first contract for the year was signed on May 17, 1848. RG 92, Records of the Office of the Quartermaster General, Register of Contracts. He had been employed previously by the army to carry express and mail.

48. Beckam has not been identified.

49. Probably Bridge Creek, sometimes called Bluff Creek. Its distance from Big John Spring is usually given as eight miles.

50. This could be either Richard Owens or F. B. Owens, both of whom took goods to Santa Fe in 1848; however, it is more probably Richard, who was a prominent Santa Fe merchant as late as 1855. Owens reached Santa Fe on July 17. *Santa Fe Republican,* July 18, 1848.

51. Dr. George East had engaged in the Chihuahua trade for many years. He was one of the Americans interned by the Mexicans for four months during the war and was liberated when Colonel Doniphan occupied the city of Chihuahua. Wislizenus, *Memoir of a Tour,* pp. 51–54.

52. This was probably Hezekiah Hoffman, a trader from Jackson, Missouri. See Barry, *Beginning of the West,* p. 665.

53. Preston Beck, a native of Indiana, was a Santa Fe merchant, at this time associated with Robert T. Brent of Virginia in the firm of Beck and Brent. Beck continued to do business in Santa Fe until 1858 when he died as a result of a knife wound received in a duel in which he killed his opponent. *Santa Fe Weekly Gazette,* April 16, 1858. Beck had arrived in St. Louis from Santa Fe on March 8 and was back in Santa Fe in July.

54. Ross and Irwin have not been positively identified. The train may have been engaged in freighting government stores under the James Brown contract. Joseph C. Irwin and E. and I. N. Ross were active in freighting over the Santa Fe Trail in the years 1849–51, but no licenses were issued in Santa Fe to anyone of these names in 1848. See Barry, *Beginning of the West*, pp. 1025–26.

55. Cornelius Davy of Independence was another of the traders who had accompanied Colonel Doniphan to Chihuahua and returned to Santa Fe at about the same time as Gibson.

56. Dr. David Waldo, a native of Virginia, entered the Santa Fe trade at least as early as 1827 and became a Mexican citizen in 1831. He served as a captain in Doniphan's regiment and participated in the invasion of Chihuahua. In 1848 he brought two trains of government stores to Santa Fe under James Brown's contract. His younger brother, Lawrence L. Waldo, was killed at Mora in the uprising of January, 1847. See James W. Goodrich, "Revolt at Mora, 1847," *New Mexico Historical Review*, XLVII (January, 1972); 51–52.

57. A cutoff from the Santa Fe Trail to Fort Leavenworth, laid out by Colonel Kearny and his dragoons in 1845, branched from the trail near Willow Spring, about ten miles southwest of the present Lawrence. It was often referred to as the Military Road.

58. James M. Hunter had for years been a trader with the Indians of what would soon be eastern Kansas and at this time, with a partner, held a license to trade with the Pottawatomies. Barry, *Beginning of the West*, p. 734.

59. Delaware (Grinter's) Ferry began operating across the Kansas River, about two miles above Shawnee Mission, probably in 1831. It was located within what was then the Delaware Indian reserve, hence the name. *Ibid.*, p. 181.

# Bibliography

*Unpublished*

Record Group 92, Records of the Office of the Quartermaster General, Register of Contracts, The National Archives, Washington, D. C.

Record Group 94, Records of the Office of the Adjutant General, Letters Received, and Orders and Special Orders, The National Archives, Washington, D. C.

Record Group 98, Records of United States Army Commands, Department of New Mexico, Letters Received, The National Archives, Washington, D. C.

Sheriff and Collectors Record of Collections and Revenues—Licenses, 1847–1867, New Mexico State Records Center and Archives, Santa Fe.

Valencia County Records, Prefect Court Record, 1847–1848, New Mexico State Records Center and Archives, Santa Fe.


*Published*

Abert, James W., *Abert's New Mexico Report, 1846–47*, Albuquerque, 1962.

Adams, Eleanor B., ed. *Bishop Tamaron's Visitation of New Mexico*, Albuquerque, 1954.

Barry, Louise, *The Beginning of the West*, Topeka, 1972.

Chávez, Angélico, "New Names in New Mexico, 1820–1850, "*El Palacio*, LXIV (September-October, 1957); 291–318.

Clarke, Dwight L., *Stephen Watts Kearny, Soldier of the West*, Norman, 1961.

Edwards, Frank S., *A Campaign in New Mexico with Colonel Doniphan*, Philadelphia, 1847.

Ferguson, Philip Gooch, "Dairy, 1847–1848," in *Marching with the Army of the West*, Ralph P. Bieber, ed., Glendale, 1936.

Frazer, Robert W., *Forts of the West*, Norman, 1965.

———— ed., *New Mexico in 1850: A Military View*, Norman, 1968.

Gibson, George Rutledge, *Journal of a Soldier under Kearny and Doniphan, 1846–1847*, Ralph P. Bieber, ed., Glendale, 1935.

Goodrich, James W., "Revolt at Mora, 1847," *New Mexico Historical Review*, XLVI (January, 1972); 49–60.

Gregg, Josiah, *Commerce of the Prairies*, Max Moorhead, ed., Norman, 1954.

Grove, Pearce S., Becky J. Barnett, and Sandra J. Hanson, eds., *New Mexico Newspapers*, Albuquerque, 1975.

Heitman, Francis B., *Historical Register and Dictionary of the United States Army*, 2 vols., Washington, D. C., 1903.

Hughes, John T., *Doniphan's Expedition*, Cincinnati, 1849.

Karnes, Thomas L., *William Gilpin, Western Nationalist*, Austin, 1970.

Lavender, David, *Bent's Fort*, Garden City, 1954.

Magoffin, Susan Shelby, *Down the Santa Fe Trail and into Mexico*, Stella M. Drumm, ed., New Haven, 1926.

Moorhead, Max, *New Mexico's Royal Road*, Norman, 1954.

Myers, Lee, "Illinois Volunteers in New Mexico, 1847–1848," *New Mexico Historical Review*, XLVII (January, 1972); 5–31.

Robinson, Jacob S., *A Journal of the Santa Fe Expedition under Colonel Doniphan*, Princeton, 1932.

Ruhlen, George, "The Battle of Brazito—Where It Was Fought," *Password*, II (May, 1957); 53–60.

*Santa Fe Republican.*

*Santa Fe Weekly Gazette.*

Sonnichsen, C. L., *Pass of the North*, El Paso, 1968.

Strickland, Rex W., "Six Who Came to El Paso: Pioneers of the 1840s," *Southwestern Studies*, I (Fall, 1963).

Taylor, Morris F., *First Mail West,* Albuquerque, 1971.

Twitchell, Ralph Emerson, *The History of the Military Occupation of the Territory of New Mexico from 1846 to 1851 by the Government of the United States,* Denver, 1909.

United States: House, *Reports of Explorations and Surveys to Ascertain the Most Practicable and Economic Route for a Railroad from the Mississippi River to the Pacific Ocean,* 33 Cong., 2 Sess., Exec. Doc. 91, 10 vols., Washington, D. C., 1855–58.

United States: Senate, *Message from the President of the United States,* 30 Cong., 1 Sess., Exec. Doc. 1, Washington, D. C., 1847.

Walker, Henry P., *The Wagonmasters,* Norman, 1966.

Webb, James J., *Adventures in the Santa Fé Trade, 1844–1847,* Ralph P. Bieber, ed., Glendale, 1931.

Wislizenus, Adolph, *Memoir of a Tour to Northern Mexico,* Albuquerque, 1969.